THE LANGUAGE OF DISTRESS
Understanding a Child's Behaviour

A. H. Brafman

KARNAC

First published in 2016 by
Karnac Books Ltd
118 Finchley Road
London NW3 5HT

British Library Cataloguing in Publication Data

A C.I.P. for this book is available from the British Library

ISBN-13: 978-1-78220-407-7

Typeset by V Publishing Solutions Pvt Ltd., Chennai, India

www.karnacbooks.com

THE LANGUAGE OF DISTRESS

CONTENTS

ACKNOWLEDGEMENTS

Considering the closeness that characterises family life, mutual understanding is vital and precious. I hope that the families described in this book would confirm my belief that our joint work was useful and helpful. I am grateful to my patients, as well as to my own family and my friends who helped me to find the way from distress to peace of mind and harmony.

ABOUT THE AUTHOR

Dr A. H. Brafman worked as a consultant child and adolescent psychiatrist in the National Health Service until his retirement. He is a qualified psychoanalyst of adults and children, and gave seminars on infant observation for trainees of the British Psychoanalytic Society and other training institutions. For many years, he ran a weekly meeting for under-fives and their parents at Queen Mary's Hospital, Roehampton, London. He has published five books based on his work with children and parents: *Untying the Knot* (Karnac, 2001); *Can You Help Me?* (Karnac, 2004); *The 5–10-Year-Old Child* (Karnac, 2010); *Fostering Independence* (Karnac, 2011), and *The Language of Drawings* (Karnac, 2012), as well as a series of papers on various clinical topics. For several years, under the sponsorship of the Winnicott Trust, he ran weekly clinical seminars for medical students at the University Hospital Medical School, Department of Psychotherapy.

INTRODUCTION

Facing a problem, we have essentially three types of reaction: some people simply follow their intuition and plunge into action, others seek advice before proceeding and a third group try to achieve a clear understanding of what is involved and only then tackle the challenge. Parenting a child is a life situation that presents no end of occasions where anxieties and fears lead to hesitations and doubts as to how to proceed. Particularly when bringing up a first child, parents often feel the pressure of wanting to help a crying baby and, yet, worry that their lack of experience might lead them to "do the wrong thing". And this is the point where the different patterns of attitudes listed above come into focus.

We have a vast literature giving advice to parents on the best way of dealing with their children. Since the middle of the last century, Dr Benjamin Spock (1946) was, for decades, the paediatrician whose views and recommendations came to represent a kind of bible, followed by parents and professionals. He succeeded in picking up virtually all types of normal and abnormal issues that parents observe when looking after their child from its birth. He gave detailed descriptions of possible developments, followed by clear advice to parents as to how they could help their child. When not successful, he urged parents to consult a professional.

Spock was a welcome alternative to Dr Truby King (Campbell, 2013), the author who had dominated the childcare stage for years. Truby King was very dogmatic; he urged mothers to feed babies strictly every four hours and, ideally, never at night. Sleeping, cuddling, and bowel movements should follow a rigid routine and babies should be kept in their rooms, though it was also important to leave them in the garden for long periods. Cuddles should never exceed ten minutes. All of this was supposed to build a baby's character and strengthen her personality.

And hundreds of books have followed, giving advice to parents on how to deal with their growing child. All of these texts have a common denominator: they describe and discuss the child's behaviour and proceed to give the parents recommendations about how to deal with any difficulty. The personality of the parents is acknowledged as an important factor, but not discussed in any detail. Good sense makes it obvious that each parent's present and past experiences are bound to influence their reaction to the child's behaviour, but this is not discussed in these books.

It was Winnicott (1991) who explicitly stressed the importance of the mother's intuition. He began his presentations in his BBC radio programmes on how to bring up your child at about the same time as Spock published his book. He did not believe in giving instructions and urged mothers to take their time and understand their babies' needs, always following and trusting their intuition: "It is when a mother trusts her judgement that she is at her best" (p. 25).

Since then, Gina Ford and Penelope Leach (Campbell, 2013) are only two of many very popular authors who have advised mothers on how to deal with their babies, and, considering the volume of sales of their books, it is obvious that many mothers read them. But at the end of the day, we are left with the need to consider the personality of the mother—not all mothers manage to trust their intuition, much as some mothers refuse to follow advice. It is also important to note that not all mothers consult books to learn how to deal with their mothering role. And we also have mothers who have to deal with their own mothers' advice, comments, and criticism! Perhaps most of them feel grateful when their husbands allow them to decide how to deal with the baby.

Clearly, all of these authors take it for granted that a baby's development is influenced by the way in which her mother deals with her.

Good sense would confirm this view, since whenever there is contact between two people, they are bound to influence and be influenced by each other, particularly when this is a prolonged contact. But watching the development of a newborn, it is not easy to determine what is part of the child's endowment and what results from the maternal input.

It is worth noting that the paediatric and psychiatric academic world has undertaken many studies to produce evidence of the effect that maternal attitudes have on the development of their child. For example, a recent paper (van Dijk et al., 2015) describes a meticulous piece of research that gives statistical evidence that "parental child-rearing attitudes are associated with functional constipation in childhood" (p. 329). Other papers, such as "The role of parenting styles in children's problem behavior" (Aunola & Nurmi, 2005) and "Functional constipation in children: does maternal personality matter?" (Farnam, 2009) add to an expansive literature that, essentially, confirms what can be clearly seen when closely observing every parent and child couple. Time goes on and formal academic research studies confirm what good sense leads us to understand.

Problem babies will lead to the health visitor being consulted and, if necessary, a referral to the paediatrician. When older children or adolescents are concerned, in our society the family's GP tends to be the first port of call if they present physical symptoms that the parents have not managed to deal with. When his physical check-up does not indicate any clear sign of organic pathology, the GP will usually recommend various ways of helping the child to overcome the symptoms involved. When these do not succeed, the GP will embark on various tests or refer the patient to a specialist. If any of these steps succeed in overcoming the symptoms, all is well and we hear no further from the family. However, if the problem persists, the last resort tends to be a referral to a psychologist or child and adolescent psychiatrist.

What follows from this referral will depend on the theoretical and technical approach of the professional consulted. For example, considering the problem of constipation, the North American Society for Pediatric Gastroenterology, Hepatology and Nutrition (Baker, Liptak, & Coletti, 2006) issued detailed recommendations on how these patients should be investigated and treated. Turning to the psychoanalytic literature, we have in Rose Edgcumbe's paper (1978) a clear and detailed study of an encopretic child, where it is the child's unconscious that constitutes the central focus of investigation. An example of how sleep disturbances are treated by a paediatrician can be seen in Kushnir and Sadeh's paper (2012).[1]

A psychoanalyst will seek to discover the *meaning* of the child's symptoms, but it seems that all other psychological professionals focus on a specific problem and proceed to apply specific techniques to overcome it or, when a young child is involved, to offer advice to the parents as to how they should help their child. I believe that the crucial point to be considered in all of these different approaches is how the child's and the parents' problem is conceptualised. Defining the child or adolescent as the patient leads to the implementation of the particular technique adopted by that professional, while seeing the parents as the carers justifies the approach where the parents are *advised* on how to help their child. But if, instead, we consider that the parents also *have* (note "have", not "are") problems that influence their approach to their child, then it becomes very important to involve them in the diagnostic and therapeutic work.

I believe that by the time the psychiatrist, psychologist, or psychodynamic worker meets the child, he faces a complex picture, where child and parents are involved in a mutually reinforcing vicious circle and it is virtually impossible to decide what is cause and what is effect. Indeed, each professional has his own preferred mode of work—the consultation may lead to advice, much as it can lead to further referrals to other professionals. Personally, I see child and parents as a unit— a group of people that influence, and are influenced by, each other.

This book describes cases where the goal was to help both child and parents to *understand* how and why they had come to be in the situation that brought them to the consultation. These were children and adolescents who presented physical problems. They had been seen by a variety of specialists who had not found any organic pathology that might explain the presenting symptoms. Several of these patients had also been referred for psychological intervention, without success. Mandy (p. 135) was seen by several specialists and had a long series of tests aiming to elucidate her persistent hip pain and abnormalities in her posture and walking. Charles's (p. 23) parents consulted various physicians and urologists regarding his compulsive, unbearable urge to urinate. Jane (p. 55) complained of visual disturbances suggestive of "a migrainous syndrome"; initial tests were normal, and it happened that before embarking on further tests and specialist consultations, the GP decided to request a child psychiatric assessment. Alex (p. 95) had severe nightmares and sleepwalking disturbances that led to several neurological consultations; no underlying physical pathology was found.

The fact that they were coming to consult me was evidence that the parents' attempts to help the child had not succeeded, and I came to realise that their interpretation of the child's behaviour was determined by personal factors and did not meet the child's actual anxieties. In fact, the fruitless efforts of the parents to help the child only reinforced the child's symptoms, because of the child feeling misunderstood and unprotected. Quite often, I found that some parents were convinced that their child had a serious physical problem and only when this misconception was clarified did the parents manage to help the child to build on his understanding of the nature of the fears that were causing his symptoms.

I eventually realised that the child's physical symptom was the external manifestation of an underlying emotionally distressing sentiment. Not being able to overcome this anxiety, the overt symptom had become the means of appealing, searching for help—a language of distress, I thought. Living with his parents, these were the ones who had to respond to the child and they could only follow what interpretation they made of the child's complaints.

Considering the result of my treatment of these cases I realised that the crucial factors leading to the disappearance of the child's symptom were: (i) the child gaining insight into the nature of his unconscious anxiety, and (ii) helping the parents to understand how they had reached their interpretation of the child's symptoms. Particularly when dealing with younger children, it is very important that the parents are able to understand the unconscious anxieties of the child and change their approach to the child.

Because of my defining the child's presenting symptoms as a language whereby he conveys his unconscious fantasies, I came to see my interpretation of his words, drawings, and behaviour as a translation: I had to find words that not only the child could understand and recognise as valid, but also that the parents could find meaningful. The same technique was applied when I was trying to discover and then show the parents how and why they had reached their unsuccessful interpretations of the child's complaints. In other words, I am depicting the consultant playing the role of a *simultaneous interpreter*. This demands that he grasps exactly what the child wants to express and this means using play materials, drawings, and formulating the right questions, until he is certain that he has learnt the content of the unconscious fantasies of that child. Similarly, he needs to ask the relevant questions to elucidate the thoughts and feelings that led the parents to decide how to respond to the child's distress.

What is required of the professional is a genuine wish to inquire, to investigate, and to discover what the child and parents are struggling with. The professional cannot ignore the information he receives from the referrers but, ideally, he must attempt to approach the child and parents as a *tabula rasa*, as if starting from zero. Indeed, all information previously obtained may guide him to ask relevant questions, but primarily, he should address the child and parents in a manner that convinces them that it is their words that he takes into account.

By definition, a medical professional considers the initial consultation as the setting where he has to reach a diagnostic evaluation of the patient, assess the probable prognoses of his findings, and explore the therapeutic options available. Most important is the decision that the presenting symptoms are either the result of a self-limited, treatable condition of recent onset or, instead, point to the presence of a more serious abnormality that may require further careful and detailed investigations.

When the patient is a child, the various therapeutic choices will require the approval and support of the parents. But in the diagnostic evaluation of the problems it is important to investigate and establish the role that the parents play in the persistence of the child's symptoms. If the child has a genetic or organic disability, the parents will be seen as carers, helping the child to cope with his difficulties. The picture is very different when the child has an acute, non-structural problem, a symptom that has eventually become part of his interaction with his parents. In this case, the parents are not only the carers but a significant factor in the persistence of the child's problems. It is this type of family dynamic that is illustrated in the cases described in this book.

I hope these reports give a clear enough illustration of this technical approach. Contrary to what happens in most psychological and medical consultations, I do not go through a series of formal questions, as if "ticking boxes"; instead, I try to convey a sincere interest in learning what child and parents consider are the difficulties they have not succeeded to resolve.

Finally, I want to make explicit my view that the technique described is not a "magic wand". When it is clear that the child requires further help, it is very important to convey this to the child and parents.

Note

1. From the abstract: "One hundred and four children aged 4–6 years with significant nighttime fears were randomly assigned into two intervention groups: the Huggy-Puppy intervention (HPI), which is based on providing children a puppy doll with a request to take care of the doll, and a revised version (HPI-r) which is based on providing the same doll with a cover story that the doll will serve as a protector."

Jeremy

Jeremy, aged three-and-a-half, was admitted to the paediatric ward of the general hospital because of a four-day history of constipation. I later had a referral letter from the paediatric registrar:

> His mother, who is very anxious, says that he has been suffering from intermittent episodes of constipation, which are precipitated by any "emotional disturbance or upset". This present episode was triggered off by the departure of Jeremy's cousin who had visited the family and left on Thursday evening. From Friday morning onwards, he refused to open his bowels. The time before this was about a month ago when he went on holiday with his mother and his father remained in England to work. Again, Jeremy refused to open his bowels, saying that his father didn't love him or care about him.
>
> His normal bowel habit is once or twice a day, but his mother says that his problem has now been going on for one-and-a-half years and she would like some psychiatric counselling. Apparently, her GP has explained that the attention that Jeremy gets from his constipation is creating a vicious circle, which he is using to manipulate his parents.

1

I spoke to the referring doctor and I found that he agreed with the mother's view that the constipation was caused by experiences of separation from people Jeremy loved. If he was versed in psychoanalytic theories, he might have phrased this idea in terms of Jeremy having such dread of being abandoned that he now treated his stools as representations of his loved objects, over which he could now exercise absolute control by retaining them inside himself. My young colleague agreed with the family doctor's view that the constipation was now being used as a weapon with which Jeremy could control his parents. This idea of children "manipulating" parents with their symptoms is very widespread. It is, in fact, an accepted way of describing the behaviour of someone who continuously approaches us with the expectation that we should relieve some distress of theirs and yet does not respond to our efforts to help them. This kind of interaction is sometimes described in psychoanalytic terms as one where we (the helpers) are made to feel the helplessness of the child/patient. However plausible this explanation may sound, it can be quite misleading, since it leads almost invariably to the maintenance of a status quo. Meeting this type of "failure", it is more productive to consider the possibility that the child/patient does not change his behaviour or find the improvement he seeks because we have failed to find the correct interpretation of what motivates the presenting complaint.

I thought that the link between constipation and separation might be correct, but it was a connection established by Jeremy's mother. Mrs J was an intelligent and sensitive mother and there would be no reason to doubt her motives in reaching this interpretation of the sequence of events in Jeremy's life and symptoms. I would still consider it very important to approach the child with an open mind regarding the unconscious meaning of his symptoms. This is not to say that the mother's information is ignored, but rather that, initially, it must be seen as a reflection of her own feelings and experiences—for example, when Mrs J mentions that Jeremy became constipated during a holiday from which his father was absent, this might be a pointer to her feelings regarding the husband's involvement with Jeremy's and/or the family's daily life.

I invited both parents to attend for an interview, together with Jeremy, but only Mrs J and Jeremy came. I saw them in an outpatient clinic where all paediatric patients attended for appointments. This clinic was run by a senior nurse whose competence I greatly admired. I took Jeremy and Mrs J to a side-room, and we sat round a table where I had put some toys, paper, and pens. I started to talk to Jeremy, as I usually do in similar meetings, intending to engage later in conversation with his mother, so as to obtain a clearer idea of how she was dealing with her child's problems. Mrs J seemed keen to tell me about herself and Jeremy, but this proved quite difficult.

I learnt only minimal information about the parents' ages and areas of work. They were both in their early thirties, pursuing professional careers. Neither of them had much experience with children and it was obvious that Mrs J found it very difficult to be firm with Jeremy, tending to give him the kind of support and understanding that showed her incapacity to impose discipline or anything which she imagined might upset him.

Jeremy's speech was not well developed. I often required Mrs J's help to understand what he had said and his vocabulary was rather limited. But he was absolutely determined to grasp my attention and ensure that I understood what he wanted to convey to me. He was smiling and his eyes shone with the hope that I would concentrate on *his* story, rather than pay attention to his mother. Jeremy picked up a pen and drew very clumsy lines, but there was no doubt that he knew exactly what each line signified (Figure 1): this was a monster, inside his castle, and he was unhappy. The squiggle in the middle of "the monster" was his "tummy", and the bottom line was a door, not to let anything come out.

Once I had learnt what was in this first drawing, Jeremy put the page aside and drew some further lines on the next page: these were quite faint[1] and apparently haphazard, but he told me that this was a church inside the castle. The monster was there and he was scared by rats that ran around. Again, he turned to another page and drew a rhinoceros. This had some birds on his head, but it also had wings to fly, "just like an elephant". I thought to myself that this unusual animal probably was part of a dream, but I said nothing, particularly as Jeremy was already turning to a new page.

He now drew again the castle, but though the page was virtually blank, he told me that there were lots of rats running in the church (he said this as if he could see them on the page) and added, as if in conclusion, that "when it comes out, it is all a mess!" I thought that I

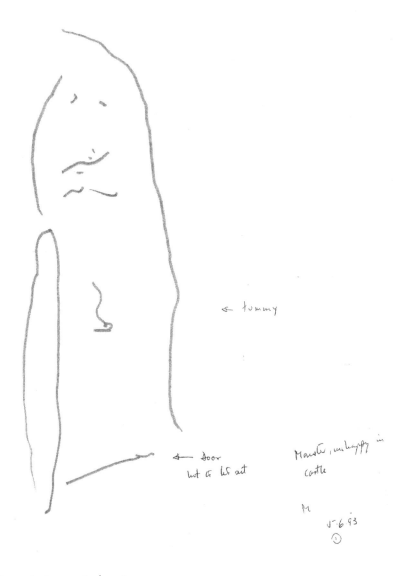

Figure 1. Jeremy's drawing.

could now voice to Jeremy my interpretation that he had shown us on paper the kind of confusion and fear that he imagined was going on inside his tummy, and that this was why he so feared letting his stools come out.

Hearing my words, Jeremy beamed, while his mother looked as if she could not quite believe her ears. And I made what turned out to be a mistake. I had become too excited by this extraordinary demonstration of a child using what means he possessed to convey the contents of his unconscious fantasies. I decided to ask Mrs J if she would permit the senior nurse in charge of the clinic to take Jeremy to the toilet. Jeremy seemed happy with this idea and Mrs J said this was quite in order, so I called in the nurse and explained what had gone on. She was quite willing to take Jeremy with her and they left us, hand in hand.

I explained in more detail to Mrs J my views as to the unconscious conflicts that Jeremy appeared to be experiencing. I said that her ideas about separation were plausible and might be very pertinent, but from Jeremy's point of view his anxiety lay in not being certain about what went on inside his body. She listened politely to my words, but she wanted to have specific advice as to how to proceed. I explained the importance of taking Jeremy to the toilet regularly, aiming at creating a rhythm that his bowels might adopt automatically, which might lead the boy to view his defecation as a normal element of his daily routine.

I was, however, disappointed to find that the nurse returned with Jeremy to report that nothing had happened. He was quite happy, none the worse for the experience, but the nurse felt she had somehow failed me, whilst I felt I had made a fool of myself. Nevertheless, Jeremy showed all the signs of having found what he had been looking for and Mrs J looked rather ill at ease, not really knowing what all this had meant. We agreed on the time and date for a further appointment, but I was intensely aware that I had acted precipitately. I had not explored Mrs J's view of the situation and there was the distinct possibility that she might take objection to my involving the nurse. I made a mental note that in the next interview I should focus more carefully on the mother's views, so that I could help Mrs J to do the nursing of her son, rather than making her feel that Jeremy could only be helped by a professional.

I could never guess what actually happened. When we next met, Mrs J told me that as soon as they had arrived home, Jeremy had asked her to go to the toilet, proceeding to defecate very normally. The same thing had happened every day afterwards. For the first two to three days, Jeremy had asked his mother to accompany him to the toilet, "in case the monsters come out", but he must have then felt confident enough, because he was able to dispense with his mother's help.

Understandably, Mrs J felt very sceptical about this development and she asked me many questions about what had taken place. Jeremy himself was very happy, playing with various toys in the room. I explained to Mrs J the significance of Jeremy's drawings and how real these fears felt to him. She understood my explanations, but it seems that this interpretation was less tangible to her than the connection she had made between constipation and life events, which she herself could imagine might be experienced as traumatic.

Mrs J did not think that we needed to make further appointments and I was kept informed of developments through speaking to the family's general practitioner over several years. Jeremy had no further constipation crises and I would interpret this as a sign that Mrs J had managed to deal with his bowel functions in a more "natural" way; that is, not as if they were a gauge of Jeremy's sense of security within the family.

Comments

It would be impossible to learn whether previous constipation episodes were also due to Jeremy's fantasy of having monsters creating havoc inside his body. However, I would assume that when Mrs J formed the idea that the constipation reflected Jeremy's anxieties over being left by someone, she would be compelled to make up for this presumed sense of abandonment. The problem now would be that of discovering how Jeremy interpreted his mother's anxious ministrations. I find it conceivable that her worries about what had happened in the outside world might reinforce Jeremy's idea that there was something inside him that gave reason for special attention. In other words, if Jeremy feared what the monster was doing inside him, Mrs J's response to his constipation would be seen as confirmation that there was reason for his worries. My belief that Mrs J had now changed her approach and treated Jeremy's bowel function "naturally" is meant to convey my idea that if he failed to pass a motion some day, this was treated as a body function that was operating in some particular way, and not as a message that Jeremy was suffering and needed special comfort, whatever form this comforting might take.

And Jeremy's drawings constitute a particularly fascinating example of how a child can find his way to convey his feelings to someone who is perceived as willing to hear and learn.

Note

1. Because this and the following two drawings are virtually invisible, they are not reprinted here.

Andrew

ndrew was nearly nine years old and had been suffering from encopresis for some three years. He also was reported to chew on rubber and a variety of other materials, and to have been preoccupied with death for quite some time. When seeing the paediatrician, his mother, Mrs A, also reported Andrew's worries about the possibility that his parents might divorce, since he had watched them having rather acrimonious rows.

The family had a very sympathetic doctor who had looked after them for many years. When Andrew was nearly eight years old, this doctor referred him to a paediatrician at their local NHS hospital. A succession of consultations followed with two child psychiatric services and another paediatrician who was covering his colleague's leave—each professional reported initially positive results, with rather early recurrence of the encopretic symptoms. Also on file was the number of failed appointments, usually leading to a new referral. Somehow, the family decided to "go private" and approached a senior child psychotherapist who lived near them. Mrs A asked to see this therapist on her own for a preliminary discussion, since she was not sure that Andrew should again be exposed to further professional consultations.

The pressure of Mrs A's questions and arguments took the therapist aback. He could recognise that she was trying to find help for a difficult problem, but each answer he gave was challenged and put back to him in a manner that he ended up thinking was too aggressive. Mrs A told the therapist about her own and her husband's jobs, which led to both of them being away from home for long periods of time. Mrs A herself was seeing a psychotherapist, though she did not mention the reason for this. After some time, she raised the question of sending Andrew to a boarding school and it emerged that this had been the main focus of her previous consultations. Much to his surprise, the therapist realised that the encopresis was being seen as a stumbling block in the parents' plan to send Andrew to boarding school, rather than as a symptom that might cause Andrew any distress. He decided that it would be unwise to take Andrew into individual psychotherapy without a preliminary assessment, both of his individual needs and of the family dynamics. At this point he asked me to see Andrew and his parents, but it was not until two months later that I was contacted by Mrs A.

Mrs A telephoned and engaged me in quite a long conversation. This virtually duplicated the points I had read in the psychotherapist's letter to me. Mrs A was fully aware that Andrew's symptom produced strong reactions in all professionals she consulted and she was keen to find it removed, but, however genuine, her concern contained an element of puzzlement about these people's reactions. It was not that she resented the fact that the messing made it difficult for Andrew to be sent to boarding school, since she tended to attribute to her husband the wish that the boy should board. It was only much later that I could recognise that, however devoted Mrs A was to Andrew, she had little understanding of how children felt in themselves. At one point, I mentioned that Andrew's self-esteem might be adversely affected by his soiling and Mrs A laughed in disbelief, as if only adults could possess such refinements of emotional experience. However, her reaction was quite sincere when she said that if I believed this was the case, she was happy to ensure that all possible help was made available to Andrew.

Both Mr and Mrs A brought Andrew to see me. He was nearly nine years old, a rather small boy, with bright, inquisitive eyes and a guarded, but friendly, smile. Mrs A looked older than I had anticipated, probably in her mid-forties, a tall lady who quickly made herself at home, perhaps seeing herself responsible for bringing the meeting together. Mr A looked older than his fifty-four years of age, a rather overweight and short man, who tried hard to disguise his displeasure at having to go through this strange experience. He was clearly a man accustomed to positions of command; he sat quietly, following the conversation whilst engaging in a rather obtrusive facial tic.

It was easy to engage Andrew in conversation. He knew the reason for seeing me and he was able to tell me about his "accidents". He felt that these occurred at any time and he attributed them to not knowing how to control his bowels and not having, therefore, time to get to the toilet. He felt ashamed afterwards, and had learnt to resort to various subterfuges in order to prevent his peers becoming aware of what had happened. He had tried to sit on the toilet and force himself to defecate, but this was seldom effective, although it was very painful when he actually managed to push some faecal mass out. He was very surprised when I asked if he also messed himself during the night. Since he knew this never happened, he had simply taken it for granted as a fact beyond questioning. He went on, in fact, to tell me of an occasion when he had woken up in the middle of the night with an urge to defecate and had ran to the toilet. Mr A interjected at this point that Andrew was leaving out the fact that from time to time he would wet the bed—a real dampener, it could be said, coming just when Andrew had found one element of self-control to report. As would become clearer later on, Mr A was a keen believer in the importance of truthfulness, and Andrew's response (an admission, followed by an apology for failing to mention it) showed he had learnt what his father expected from him.

Andrew told me about his life at school and at home. He came across as an intelligent boy, able to engage in relationships both with peers and teachers. He had changed schools because Mrs A had not been happy with the teachers in his first school, but Andrew had taken the change in his stride. He had a younger sister, aged six, and he described a relationship between them that seemed quite unremarkable. He had no difficulty speaking about friends and neighbours, but when it came to the actual messing, he found himself quite at a loss for words. I said that I wanted to speak to his parents about the history of the family and invited him to make a drawing—he was happy to do this and took up a seat by a desk in my room.

When I asked Mr A if he could tell me something about himself, he made a face; I could not decide whether this expression reflected puzzlement, annoyance, or contempt. I explained that I would be better able to understand Andrew's problem if I had some idea of the background in which he had grown up. He seemed to accept this and told me about his working life. He had worked for a large company for many years, occupying positions of increasing importance. After several years in a particularly taxing post, he suddenly found himself transferred to the main office, where he got into conflict with his new bosses. After months of arguments over policy and philosophy of work, Mr A left the company. Soon afterwards, he saw an advert for another international firm and decided to apply for it. He was given this job, which again involved long periods away from home, but his work provided him enormous satisfaction.

I asked Mr A about his life outside of work. He had been married before and told me of the children from that marriage, saying they were "just as intelligent as the two I have now, but only one of them is prepared to work hard". From the information he gave, and particularly from the inflections of his voice, it was clear that Mr A considered intelligence a prerequisite for respect, but if it was not accompanied by dedication and high moral standards, intelligence was not even a reason for mitigation of his antagonism. I would guess his enemies might say he opposed or dismissed anyone who did not agree with him, but there was no way of checking on such an idea. I was interested to note that Mr A's facial tic disappeared when he became more involved in the conversation.

Mrs A was the youngest child in a large family and she had virtually no experience of children until Andrew was born. After graduating from university she had joined the same company where her husband worked and, in fact, had worked directly with him for several years before and after they were married. She had stayed in the company after her husband left and she seemed very involved in her work. Her father had died many years ago, and when I asked about her mother Mrs A answered that she "was awful", and both she and her husband laughed. It emerged that both of them felt their mothers were dismal failures—one because she was too chaotic, the other because she was too obsessive and demanding.

Throughout the conversation, Andrew kept on with his colourful drawing, which could not be seen from where we were sitting. Occasionally, he would interject some word or comment, such as when his parents hesitated about naming someone or remembering where some relation lived. But when we talked about the grandparents, Andrew became more alert, particularly when the parents told me about his paternal grandfather.

This grandfather had been Andrew's idol. He had always devoted long hours to Andrew and they shared a passion for model airplanes. He had been ill for five months, so the family had felt relieved when he died, but Andrew was often taken to see him in hospital and, up until the last week of his life, Andrew and his grandfather had built airplanes together. His death had occurred some three years ago. When I asked Andrew how he felt, he said "sad ... very sad". Both parents reacted with surprise, saying that they had wondered many times why it was that Andrew had seemed not to have felt anything about his grandfather's death. We all looked at him, and Andrew explained that he understood their surprise: "I didn't show it ... I was sad only when I was in my room".

Both parents were shaken by Andrew's explanation. I decided not to put into words the obvious interpretation that Andrew must have learnt long ago that his parents could not take in someone's feelings of pain. Instead, I asked Andrew if he knew how to recognise when his parents were sad. To their surprise, he said an emphatic "yes" and explained that he knew his mother was sad "when she looks like she looks now"—and, indeed, Mrs A looked quite miserable. She smiled, embarrassed, but made no comment. What about Mr A, I asked. Andrew claimed that he could recognise his sadness, but was not able to articulate how he does this.

Surprisingly, it was Mrs A who put the dates together and suddenly asked aloud if it was possible that the grandfather's death might have any connection with Andrew's soiling, seeing that both had occurred "three years ago". Andrew looked quite surprised, but said nothing. Mr A now told me that, at the time of his father's death, Andrew had pleaded to be allowed to attend the funeral, but it was decided that he should not go. He said that Andrew would still, to this day, refer back to the death of his grandfather and to the fact that he was not allowed to attend the funeral. I said that something must be upsetting Andrew about those events and that he might find it difficult to put into words what that would be. However, it was possible that his drawing might contain some answer to these questions, since he had been working on it all through our conversation. I asked Andrew to tell us what he had drawn and, as he began to describe the drawing, I suggested that both parents should come nearer the desk, so that they could see the picture.

Andrew had drawn (Figure 2) a very colourful Spitfire firing at a German plane. He had already hit another German and this meant that when he returned to base, and if his story was confirmed, he would be given a Swastika to stick to his plane. Somehow, both Mr and Mrs A were shocked by this and asked what had happened to the German pilot. "Oh, he escaped—he jumped out just in time, when the plane was going down in flames—he was only half-burnt."

At this point, we had one of those unusually clear examples where we can say that one unconscious established contact with another unconscious. Mr A now told me that it might be relevant to mention that his father had been cremated. Obviously, this information brought dramatic poignancy to the drawing showing the German

Figure 2. Andrew's drawing.

plane plunging down, with a black cloud of smoke behind it, but with an empty cockpit. It was probably not necessary to put into words what had been Andrew's anxiety: that his beloved grandfather might have survived, through escaping, half-burnt, from his cremation. In other words, Andrew still believed that he might have accepted the death and loss of his grandfather if he had been allowed to watch his actual cremation.

Andrew looked relieved. His parents appeared quite stunned as they returned to their seats. I thought I should sum up our meeting and I told them that, to my mind, the soiling was both a habit that needed steps to be corrected and that it had now become Andrew's way of crying for his grandfather. We all saw Andrew nodding vigorously as I was saying this. But Mr and Mrs A, in total disbelief, asked him, in unison, whether he really agreed with what I had said. "Yes", said Andrew. Mr A was not satisfied and asked again, "Do you mean 'yes'?" and Andrew repeated, now much louder, "yes!"

I told Mr and Mrs A that they had to give Andrew further help to get his bowels to create a regular rhythm and suggested they should get him to sit on the toilet regularly every morning and evening, until it became clear which was the best time to empty his bowels. I also suggested a points system,[1] so that Andrew felt some additional encouragement to achieve control of his sphincters. When he reached a total they could agree on, he was to be given a reward.

I was going on leave one week later, so we arranged that they would telephone and report on Andrew's progress. When no call came, I phoned them myself. Andrew had scored full points that week: he had been both dry and clean. Mrs A sounded pleased as she told me this. We arranged that she would call me after my return from leave, so that we could discuss if any further help was needed; again, I heard nothing from her. I wrote asking for news, and also sending my invoice, but received no reply. After another letter, I telephoned the family again. Mrs A apologised for not settling my bill and promised to do so "tomorrow". But the good news was that Andrew had remained dry and clean—until that very week of my telephone call. Mrs A said she could not think of any reason for this "accident". However, almost immediately, she asked me what I thought of the plan to send Andrew to boarding school. With as much care as I could muster, I answered that there was a possibility that the resurgence of the soiling might be related to this plan.

I raised the question of individual psychotherapy, emphasising that this would help Andrew to gain a better understanding of how his bodily functions had become a means of expressing his feelings. But Mrs A, very sweetly, pointed out various difficulties that would not allow the family to support such a venture at that point. It seemed quite obvious that the decision had already been made that Andrew should be sent to boarding school. I enquired about another appointment with me, but Mrs A said that this was not really convenient at that point in time.

Comments

I think it would be impossible to establish how or why Andrew became enuretic or encopretic. Perhaps if he went into individual psycho-therapy, this might eventually elucidate the original meaning of these symptoms, but at the time of my consultation it was quite obvious that both sphincter dysfunctions had become the expression of Andrew's feelings about the manner in which his parents treated him. The ques-tion of professional fees is not usually brought into clinical papers, but here was a wealthy family who appeared to have treated me in a man-ner that may well have born some similarity to how they treated their son. After telling me that she would settle my account "tomorrow", Mrs A did not do so. I sent two further letters, at monthly intervals, with no success. Only when the family received official notice of court proceedings did Mrs A telephone to apologise and then send me the cheque for my fees. It is this kind of pseudo-correctness and attention that must have tormented Andrew in his failed attempts to get him-self heard by his parents. Follow-up information came from the family doctor. Andrew did go to boarding school and apparently did quite well there. The doctor did not have detailed information and she could only tell me that, after seeing me, the family had not requested further help for Andrew.

Looking back, it does seem that boarding school was the best option for this boy. It must have been quite painful for him to find his enuresis and encopresis disappearing for several weeks, only to discover that its resurgence did not lead to the kind of help that had been so effective, but rather to some *status quo ante* response—as if nothing had happened that might have upset him.

Note

1. When recommending a reward system, I stress that this must follow a "strict business deal" model and I generally give the family an idea that they may decide to follow. With Andrew, I suggested giving him two points if he was clean at the end of the day and one point if he remained dry overnight—but also deducting two and one points if an "accident" occurred. A prize is decided on at the beginning of the scheme, to match an agreed total of points.

Thomas

Thomas was twelve when I saw him with his mother. He was referred by the family doctor, who wrote:

> Thomas has never been dry at night. He has no daytime problems. He is apparently happy at home and school. He has two sisters (aged one and eleven) and a seventeen-year-old brother at a residential college; this latter child has spina bifida and is doubly incontinent, although Mrs T says "this has never been an issue". He can walk with sticks.
>
> Thomas has taken amitriptyline 50 mg nocte, but this did not help and neither did attendance at an enuresis clinic two and four years ago. He has made some improvement on desmopressin 20 micrograms (two puffs) nocte, but the problem recurred when the spray ran out.

Mrs T was a sensitive, attractive, and very articulate young woman. She spoke with a firm tone of voice, but this was not cold or distant. Thomas was perhaps small for his age, but he was obviously a healthy child, very intelligent and well-attuned to the people around him. He was immensely ill at ease when we first met; I thought, in fact, that he was plainly afraid of me. I asked him several questions, but he could only muster monosyllables. As I asked him about the family structure, Thomas seemed to find this easier, with Mrs T joining in to confirm or clarify any information that led me to indicate some degree of surprise.

It was not just that the family appeared to have an unusual configuration, but that pain seemed to be a recurring element in its development. The father of the oldest child had left Mrs T shortly after his birth, presumably because he could not cope with the pain of nursing a handicapped child. Thomas's father apparently had managed to look after both his own children and the first son of his wife, but then he also left the family shortly after Mrs T had to undergo an operation for a skin cancer. The youngest child was born from a new relationship that Mrs T had formed some time later.

Thomas was well aware of all these events. He would occasionally throw in some remark, adding something to his mother's account. When, for example, Mrs T was describing the problems they have when the oldest son is at home, she mentioned that he would at times hit his head against the wall in a compulsive manner, as if immune to pain. This behaviour had decreased over the years, but here Thomas added that his brother had now developed the habit of pulling his hair out. Throughout this account, Thomas was crying painful tears. I was reminded of the doctor's comment ("this has never been an issue"), apparently quoting Mrs T, but I limited myself to acknowledging how upset Thomas was by his brother's condition. I do not know whether his tears had surprised Mrs T, but she certainly made no comment about this.

Mrs T told me of her operation four years earlier. She stressed the trauma of her husband leaving her by mentioning the days of the week on which the operation was carried out and of his departure five days later. As she recounted the details of these events, I was surprised to see how much she seemed to be taking for granted that this was already known by Thomas. He did not interrupt or correct her, but his face clearly showed how upset he was by those events. After all, it was his father who was being discussed, and he was not depicted as a devoted or even loyal spouse. Mrs T also described his treatment of the children as quite despicable.

I tried to focus on Thomas's wetting. This time, he was more receptive and openly voiced his sense of helplessness and his disbelief that he would ever overcome this problem. Listening to him, I was in no doubt that he saw his enuresis as being of the same nature as his brother's incontinence, hence his conviction that it was beyond correction. Because I thought he would value being treated as a thinking person, I decided to show him the connection between the various parts of the urinary system. He followed this with total concentration and fascination. When I mentioned that there were two sphincters (children love this word, which they can never spell—they visibly log it for their next game of hangman or Scrabble), one voluntary and one involuntary, he could immediately grasp the fact that if his wetting only occurred at night, this meant that his voluntary sphincter was absolutely normal. Thomas was visibly relieved upon realising this.

My main surprise came when I asked Thomas if he had any idea about why he wet his bed. He was the only child I have ever seen who answered that this was probably related to his "having many worries on [his] mind". After all of our conversation, it seemed appropriate and timely to say that his wetting was a form of crying—he agreed that this seemed to be the case.

Mrs T wanted to know how to proceed. Should she continue to give Thomas his spray? Did I believe in all the various recommendations they had collected over the years (and she quoted a few)? I suggested that she should explore the minimal effective dose of desmopressin and that she should investigate the time when Thomas usually wets his bed, as she might try to wake him up just before that time. Finally, I endorsed her idea that he should restrict his fluid intake toward the end of the day.

Thomas had said that he would like to talk to someone about his feelings, so I offered him sessions with the clinic's child psychotherapist. At our next appointment three weeks later, Thomas came with a diary to show me how the episodes of wetting had decreased and that he had now had a run of over one week of dry nights. But this was, undoubtedly, a joint triumph; Thomas was now using only one puff (he was keen to mention that just half a puff had also worked on one occasion), and Mrs T had undertaken to wake him up just before the time when he appeared to wet himself: she had started to call him at 3 a.m. but, having found him already wet, she had proceeded to call him at 2 a.m.

We discussed these patterns and I suggested that Mrs T should attempt to increase the intervals between micturitions, as this would reinforce Thomas's feeling that he had his bladder under control. They came to see me again one month later and they both felt Thomas had overcome his wetting. The desmopressin had been reduced to virtually nothing and Mrs T was now risking not calling Thomas during the night. He seemed confident that all was well. I reminded them of the psychotherapist, wanting to apologise for our running a waiting list, but both Thomas and his mother said this was no longer necessary.

We did not make further appointments, leaving them the option to approach me again, if necessary.

Comments

Both Thomas and his mother felt crushed by their sense of hopelessness. When I tried to voice some sympathetic comment to Mrs T about the amount of pain she had already experienced in her life, she limited herself to say that her mother had always been very supportive. I interpreted this as indicating that: (i) she expected no solutions, only comfort; and (ii) she had no desire to get involved with strangers (therapists?).

When Thomas suddenly realised that he had no irreversible physical handicap, I believe that both he and his mother realised that they stood the chance of facing one battle that they could actually win. The only translation required for an unconscious feeling was my comment about the wetting representing tears. That this resulted from Thomas's identification with his brother, and that Mrs T had considered Thomas's wetting as incurable, as happened with his brother, was left unspoken—and yet, subsequent events showed quite conclusively that they had managed to overcome this misidentification. Mrs T was able to believe that she could offer effective help and Thomas managed to regain control of his body. Finally, this improvement could be sustained because Mrs T was able to disengage and allow Thomas to enjoy his self-sufficiency. For me, this was a very gratifying, beautiful, and moving case.

Charles*

Sixteen-year-old Charles came to see me with his parents. His family doctor has asked me to see him because he was still enuretic and this made for great difficulties in his school and general social life. The interview lasted two hours and it would be impossible to convey in detail how each participant contributed to the discussion—it was very lively and easy-going, moving from the formal to the "jokey", with many unexpected discoveries which gave rise to amusement just as often as to shock and pain. Charles was a well-built adolescent with no particular distinguishing features. He was reasonably intelligent, not very articulate, and quite shy—perhaps only too aware of the circumstances in which he was seeing me. His parents were an ordinary working-class couple, laughing and talking with the respect they would show a doctor, and yet with the warmth and ease they might express when meeting neighbours or friends.

I first tried to get Charles to tell us how he saw his problems. In a voice loaded with embarrassment, he said that he was still wetting his bed. He had tried many medications and various techniques, and had

---

*Previously published in *Untying the Knot* (Brafman, 2001).

recently had some slight improvement when he was given imipramine, but the wetting still continued. He explained how this affected his social life—never accepting invitations to stay at friends for the night or going on school outings, for example. To the best of his knowledge, he had never had any periods when he was dry at night. I presume he considered my response sympathetic enough, because he seemed to gain courage to add that he had an additional problem, in that during the day he felt every so often an urge to urinate, which was so pressing that he had to leave the classroom or interrupt any activity to avoid wetting himself.

Mr and Mrs C told me that they were quite aware of Charles's problem. Initially, they simply acknowledged its existence, but gradually they embarked on accounts of the way in which this urinary frequency affected their family life. From stories about meal times being interrupted, they moved to a description of journeys by train or car; by this point the psychiatric social worker and I were laughing as much as all of them were. Car journeys would be interrupted "every two miles" and the family would wait until Charles found a suitable place to urinate; they sometimes missed train connections while waiting for Charles to find a toilet. The wider family had always made jokes out of the recurrent lateness that characterised the Cs' visits. We were told in great detail, and with considerable laughter, how the parents and Charles's sister would stay at the door, waiting for Charles to feel satisfied that he had emptied his bladder, before he managed to join them so they could leave home.

It was quite difficult to find a way to shift from this comedic atmosphere to the painful implications of Charles's problem. I asked the parents about how they had come to accept the incredible manoeuvres they performed in order to fit in with Charles's needs. I was promptly put in my place: how could a parent behave any differently vis-à-vis a needy child? And they gave me other examples of how they dealt with their children's lives—they obviously did not distinguish between a wish and a need, and they painted a picture of the children being left to find their own way in life, as if any imposition or demand on the parents' part would represent an intrusion to be avoided. Firmness or discipline seemed taboo and, to an outsider, Mr and Mrs C seemed to have fostered a domestic climate that could not but lead to a chaotic style of life. Nevertheless, when we talked about Charles's younger sister, it seemed that she had flourished in this same atmosphere. She was described as efficient, neat, task-oriented, and invariably successful at school and other areas of her life. For some reason, Charles's problems had only become a rigid routine within the interaction he had developed with his parents.

I tried to explore with Charles how he experienced his problems. It turned out that he was totally convinced that there was some anatomical fault in his urinary apparatus. Considering his age and the fact that he had studied some biology at school, I asked him to describe his image of what micturition involved. Not surprisingly, he did not know about bladder sphincters, let alone about voluntary and involuntary functions. We focused on the kidneys, bladder, and penis. Charles knew that, however frequent and overwhelming his urge to urinate, he had never actually wet himself during the day. Gradually, he realised that this fact indicated that there could not be any organic defect underlying his symptoms. And suddenly he was not just relieved—he was enthusiastic.

Mr and Mrs C followed our conversation with some interest, though they looked quite puzzled, as if not quite seeing how it could be relevant. I had noticed that they were shifting their positions on their chairs, as if finding it difficult to understand why they had to be kept in the room. Indeed, Mr C eventually could not contain himself any longer and, with the tone of voice one associates with a little schoolboy addressing the class-teacher, he asked me for permission to leave the room to smoke a cigarette, since he had "not had a cigarette for some three hours now!" Well, this was an unexpected demonstration of the fact that Charles was not the only one to struggle with urges and self-control. At this point, having noticed how overweight Mrs C was, it became very difficult not to consider that she also struggled with the same difficulty to impose control over physical urges. I did manage to voice a comment on the similarity between Mr C's request and Charles's demands that the family should stop the car along the motorway, but I thought it would not be wise (or prudent?) to remark on Mrs C's weight.

But Mr C's decision to smoke his cigarette led us to discuss the fundamental issue of what is and is not acceptable. This interview took place many years before smoking became such a condemnable habit as it is nowadays, but the very fact that Mr C had asked me for permission underlined the point that one person's need may impinge on another one's views. This was the much-needed cue to look at the parents' attitudes towards Charles's urinary problems. Now, however, Mr and

Mrs C showed a different facet of their personalities: they felt accused and became quite angry that they might be found at fault. I tried to show that there was no question of allocating blame, but Charles took over. This was now suddenly a self-confident youngster, as if he had at last found it possible to let us know that he had thoughts and opinions of his own.

Charles argued that what his parents thought was kindness and tolerance towards his wetting and frequency had in fact led to his being confused about it. "If a child goes about the house scribbling on the walls, you would expect the parents to teach the child that that kind of behaviour is not acceptable!" I thought Mrs C understood Charles's argument, but Mr C was quite dumbfounded by this, as if the meaning of Charles's words had escaped him and only the notion of "an outburst" (i.e., another episode of incontinence) counted to him.

Charles looked pleased. Perhaps he found it gratifying that the psychiatric social worker and I seemed to have "taken his side", even if his parents appeared not to have understood his grievances. But Mr and Mrs C felt they needed something more tangible to take away with them. They asked for a prescription—what should they do? How should they respond to Charles? I was only a new doctor, coming on the scene after a long list of physicians and specialists, who had conducted innumerable tests and examinations, and my intervention was only talking? What could this achieve?

I was quite determined to keep away from the model of "illness", believing that now to behave "like a doctor does" would only lead Charles to fall back on the notion of there being "something wrong with his body". Furthermore, I did not really think that these parents, however devoted and loving they undoubtedly were, would be able to change their approach to Charles. I thought that I had to concentrate on helping Charles to build up his self-confidence and I asked the parents to forgive me if I did not give them any definite recommendation. I suggested they should just think over all the things we had discussed and I asked Charles to come and see me again. However, I asked him to make a diary, noting which nights he had a wet bed.

Charles came to see me three weeks later. Mrs C also came along. Charles had counted twenty nights without "accidents" and both he and his mother were very happy with this. Mrs C was particularly proud and she stressed how much Charles had gained in confidence as the days had gone by. He was more outgoing, his tone of voice showed more firmness, he was seeing much more of his peers, and, altogether, he seemed happier. Charles beamed at all this praise.

Charles came to see me once more, a month after our second meeting. This time, he could barely disguise his reluctance to attend. He now counted thirty-six consecutive nights without any wetting, and only one accident—followed by a further twenty-four dry nights. These figures were put forward as if they were jewels or trophies; they obviously meant an enormous amount to him. He now expected the final verdict to come from me, and I had no doubt that the best prize would be for me to confirm that he could now proceed on his own. We parted with a warm handshake, and Charles knew he could see me again—if, only if, this was necessary (i.e., if he ever wished to do so).

It was only from the general practitioner that I learnt, some months later, that Charles had not had any further urinary problems.

Comments

Contrary to what happened in other cases, I did not learn of any unconscious fantasies that Charles might have construed about his symptoms, except for his conviction of having some physical damage. Understanding that this fault was non-existent sufficed to remove his anxiety. This case illustrates the power of family dynamics to create features round an original symptom that dramatically affects an individual member of that family. Assuming that the C family had problems over impulse control, we might postulate that Mrs C's weight and Mr C's smoking represented manifestations of this conflict. However, it seemed that they did not consider these features as pathological, but when Charles built his own complex of compulsive behavioural symptoms around his urination, this became the focus of the family concerns. I am sure that our meetings led to no change in each parent's behaviour, but Charles managing to free himself from his symptom enabled him to build his self-image and self-confidence and develop a more "age-appropriate" life pattern—and his being a late adolescent this would have contributed to his taking a step forward to his independence and self-sufficiency.

Paul

The paediatric consultant asked me to see Paul when he was three years old because the boy's constipation had not responded to various drug treatments. When he first saw Paul, the paediatrician prescribed a programme of laxatives and diet, besides giving Mrs P detailed instructions as to how to help her son achieve a regular rhythm of emptying his bowels. At the second follow-up appointment, the mother's report produced intense alarm in the paediatrician. At one level of dosage, the drugs were producing "a powerful evacuation", with such mess that the mother felt this was unfair on Paul. At a smaller dosage, however, Paul was again holding back his stools, so that Mrs P had now "arranged the situation so that every third day she put Paul in the bath and encouraged him to empty his bowels into it". The paediatrician thought this was not a case for a simple change of medicines, and tried to convince Mrs P that making Paul defecate in the bath was unhygienic and educationally undesirable. Mrs P said she might agree with the hygiene aspect, but not otherwise. I do not really know how the discussion went, but eventually the paediatrician managed to persuade Mrs P that she should consult a child psychiatrist. Reluctantly, Mrs P agreed to see me.

Paul had achieved his developmental milestones quite normally and by the age of eighteen months was dry and clean. Some time after that, Paul began to show a reluctance to empty his bowels and Mrs P turned to health visitors and doctors in search of effective advice. Various drugs and diets were tried. Paul was kept in nappies and encouraged to empty his bowels into them. Progress charts with various rewards were attempted, but the problem persisted. In due course, the boy had been referred to the consultant paediatrician, who had now asked me to see Paul.

At our first meeting, I was told a very unusual and sad family history. Mr P was in his late forties and had three children from a previous marriage. His work involved travelling abroad and his contact with Paul was rather limited. Mrs P was thirty-eight years of age. She had been married to a man who was keen to have children, but they had not managed to have any. At one point, after she had a brief affair, the couple decided to separate, but Mrs P soon discovered she was pregnant. She was thrown into great emotional turmoil, since she barely knew the man whose child she was now carrying. In a painful meeting with her husband, he pleaded with her to continue to live with him, as they would now have the child they wanted so much. But, after much thought, she decided the child should live with his real father and left her husband. Sadly, however, having married Mr P, the new couple had never managed to build a stable relationship and there were increasing difficulties in their marriage.

As I tend to do in all cases of bowel dysfunction, I enquired about the parents' bowel habits. It turned out that neither Mr nor Mrs P "paid much attention" to this; both just assumed that their bowels opened every second or third day. As for Paul, Mrs P told me how he would curl up on his belly in a "frog position", tightening up his legs; she believed this was his way of ensuring that the faeces would not come out. Occasionally he would sit on the potty and defecate normally.

Paul had quickly made himself at home in my room. He explored several toys, he smiled to me in a friendly manner, not giving many answers to my questions, but clearly making sure I was paying attention to his activities. He picked up some felt-tip pens and made some clumsy scribbles, but he soon was banging the crayons and making a loud noise that (he instructed me) I was supposed to jump at. Each time I jumped, he laughed, pleased and excited, only to repeat the game again. After a while, he stopped and moved away to the dolls' house; he was now quite silent, perhaps following the conversation I was having with his mother.

Mrs P had never had any experience with children before her son was born. She was a caring and loving mother, but she only knew to take into account Paul's behaviour, much as she did with his words, at face value. Mrs P just did not believe that Paul's play might have any meaning or that he might have feelings and thoughts that, at his age, he lacked the capacity to articulate. When I tried to suggest that Paul's sphincter difficulties might be linked to his feelings and ideas, rather than to some physical factor that required diet and/or medication, she reacted with polite scepticism. After so many attempts at medical intervention that had invariably failed, she was willing to consider new clinical evaluations, but she could not agree with the idea that the workings of a child's body might be significantly influenced by his feelings.

I searched for some example that might convince Mrs P. I remembered Paul's game, demanding I should jump when he made his noisy "bangs"; I suggested to his mother that those were the noises he feared his stools would make. Paul promptly pronounced a very clear "Yes!", but Mrs P argued, kindly but firmly, that he could not possibly have heard any noises, since "there was no bang" when he used the potty, the water, or the nappy. I laughed and admitted she must be right, but it was still possible that Paul might have heard someone else or even heard an unrelated noise or, who knows?, simply imagined a connection between faeces and noise—the fact remained that he had confirmed my suggestion. Mrs P could admit this, but she was not convinced.

We had run out of time and I discussed with Mrs P the importance of sitting Paul on the toilet and trying to achieve a situation where he might develop a habit of defecating which would not be connected to fears or ideas of any kind. She asked me about drugs and I said this was something she must discuss with the paediatrician. Mrs P was puzzled by the whole interview, but said she "would try".

I saw Paul and his mother again two weeks later. Both of them looked more relaxed, but there had not been any significant progress. Mrs P and I sat on the same chairs we had occupied the previous time and Paul explored the toys in the room. He took up some trains and the rails on which they could move; he built a circuit, putting a tunnel at one point and began to make the trains move. He then built a smaller circle, retaining the tunnel, and now moved the little carriages, getting them to crash and making loud noises with his mouth. Time and again, a carriage would get stuck inside the tunnel and this made Paul pick up a ruler nearby and then make "strenuous" and loud efforts to push the train out of the tunnel. Mrs P said Paul "enjoys the noise". Again, Mrs P was focusing on the overt behaviour and emphasising the mechanical aspect of Paul's play. I was keen to help Paul convey to his mother what was troubling him and to achieve this I had to translate what I believed was the communication Paul was depicting through his play with the trains. Being careful to use a gentle tone of voice, I suggested to Mrs P that the circle and the tunnel might be a representation of Paul's idea of an anus. Mrs P was taken aback, but promptly and quietly asked Paul "is that your bottom?", to which he said "yes". In view of his confirmation, I pointed out how he kept getting a train stuck inside the tunnel and then making exaggerated efforts to push it out. I stressed the "stuck inside" and the "forcing out", adding that he was illustrating his anxiety about what happened inside himself and his fear of what would come out of him. Here, we had an unexpected change. To my surprise, Mrs P told me of a children's story which Paul keeps asking her to read to him: the story of "Henry the engine", a locomotive that gets stuck in a tunnel. Each time she gets to this point, Paul becomes anxious and distressed, asking her how will Henry manage to come out.

There was no doubt that Mrs P had finally seen the link between Paul's play with the trains, the story he asked her to read, his reaction to the story, and the trouble he had with allowing his stools to come out of his body. Mrs P looked relieved and Paul was clearly pleased with finding that his game had been translated into words. Mrs P wanted to stay on the safe side and, in spite of her understanding, she still requested a definite plan to put into practice. We discussed making a chart of Paul's progress, his success earning him "a metal ball", which he was keen to have. I emphasised that it was important not to ask Paul about going to the toilet, but rather to take him there at the same time each day, so that his body could develop its own rhythm of functioning.

Mrs P did not wish to make another appointment at that point and we arranged that she would let me know of Paul's progress. Two months later, Mrs P reported that Paul had now developed a regular rhythm where he defecated every second day, without requiring any drugs. To my surprise, she added that he was still occasionally wetting his bed, something I had not been told before. I urged Mrs P to attend again, but she refused this, saying that Paul would "just grow out of it" in due course. I had to accept that Mrs P could not appreciate that Paul might be as much distressed by his enuresis as he had been about his constipation. From a prognostic point of view, this did not augur too well for Paul's development, but it was just possible that he might manage to achieve bladder control, even if without the support of his parents.

Comments

Mrs P did not consult the paediatrician again, but I heard from the general practitioner that Paul seemed to have maintained control of his bowel movements. The consultation had shown that Paul had found in his play a language whereby he could express the nature of his unconscious anxieties, but it was sad that his mother seemed unable to recognise how valuable this capacity of his was. Like Mrs J (Jane's mother: see p. 55), Mrs P was also not prepared to accept any other than verbal expressions of the child's thoughts and feelings. I am sure that this must be a very important factor in what Winnicott called "the false self" (1960), where the child learns and adapts to the mother's capacities and learns that certain thoughts and feelings can only be expressed through physical symptoms, specific types of behaviour, or not at all.

Paul is a wonderful example of how a child seems to come to the consultation as if with his homework prepared. I do believe that this occurs very often, but it is not that easy for the consultant to pick up the cues given by the child. The only guideline I follow results from my conviction that the child wants to get rid of his problem and assesses this stranger, considering whether he or she might be a potential helper. If the professional meets that expectation, the child "opens up", and then it becomes a matter of the professional looking for cues that might relate to the symptom, as it is perceived, experienced by the child. This is how I explain, for example, my taking Paul's banging of his toys with increasing intensity as a rendering of the noise that his stools might make—a mixture of excitement and fear.

I failed to understand how Mrs P could help Paul overcome his phobia of the toilet and then refuse to attempt a similar approach regarding his wetting. This could well be due to her objecting to my technique, but it could also result from her difficulty in seeing Paul gaining further independence from her ministrations. Unfortunately, I had no opportunity to explore these possibilities.

Claude

C laude was three years old when he was referred to a consultant paediatrician during a visit to his grandparents and this doctor wrote the following report for the family's usual GP.

Claude seems to have been a lively and happy boy until the parents returned from a three-week holiday three months ago. A few days after coming home, his mother tried to get Claude to come out of nappies and use the potty, but despite running around with the bare bottom he would not use the toilet and withheld urine until he had pants on later, at which point he wet himself. After a few days of this behaviour, Claude became emotionally distraught, listless, anorectic and just wanting to go to bed. He was also clingy and difficult when he started screaming at night. There had been no obvious reason why Claude would not use the toilet or potty: no frights or negative enforcement and he had seen his parents and older sister using the toilet. He would not even urinate outside in the garden, wanting to hide in the corner with pants on before he would do it. Since this time, Claude's behaviour has really changed quite a lot. He is now emotionally labile with tantrums. He easily becomes distressed and will not go to other people. A neighbour tried to help with the potty training and Claude is said to have become completely hysterical. His mother has been particularly concerned about it because of the lassitude and poor appetite with weight loss.

After a thorough physical examination that excluded any pathology, the doctor recommended, "we should forget about potty-training for the moment" and suggested that the GP might want to refer Claude to a "clinical psychologist, mostly so that Mrs C has reassurance about the way she manages Claude and to plan for re-establishing potty-training".

The paediatrician had obviously taken great care to assess the situation and his views are quite typical of similar consultations. Physically, nothing can be found; the child is reacting to some traumatic experience, but has now developed a behaviour problem and, therefore, the mother must be helped to cope with her unnecessary worries, which should enable her to put the child back on the track of normal development. This doctor gave good advice, since "forgetting about potty-training for the moment" was bound to reduce the vicious circle of unhappiness, failure, and pain in which child and mother had become caught up. As for the recommendation to "refer to a clinical psychologist", this reflects the belief that only "wrong" or "faulty" behaviour is at stake and that this would be corrected through some form of retraining.

The family's general practitioner wrote in his referral letter to the Child Guidance Clinic:

> A very distraught parent came to see me, as since she attempted to potty train her child some six weeks ago, which was a total disaster, the child's behaviour has become impossible and he is rejecting all normal convention, despite the parents showing no concern regarding the failure of the training programme.

Reading this letter I wondered whether "parents showing no concern" was really compatible with "a very distraught parent came to see me".

Mrs C brought Claude to see me. She was an attractive, not so young person, clearly self-confident, and treating Claude warmly and sensitively. Claude was quite a small boy, and very shy; he was absolutely fascinated by a young, blonde psychologist who worked with me and could not get his eyes away from her. I asked Mrs C how she had told

Claude about our meeting and she could not see the relevance of the question, simply telling me that she had told him they were coming "to see the doctor". The psychologist asked Claude some questions and he mumbled monosyllables in reply.

I had put pens and paper on a table, together with a dolls' house and some toys, and Claude moved towards the pens. Mrs C happily began to tell us the story described in the consultant's letter and one could sense the intensity of the feelings of distress that both Claude and his mother had experienced. While his mother was talking to us, Claude began to play with the pens, naming each colour, and then making some lines, which looked more like smudges, on one of the sheets of paper. At one point, he made an "L", saying this was his sister's, Louise's, letter (Figure 3). Mrs C corrected him, as he had made this "L" the "wrong way round", but Claude ignored her comment.

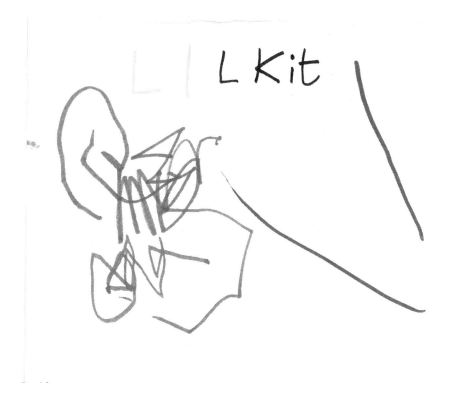

Figure 3. Claude's first drawing.

Claude now took another sheet of paper (Figure 4) and drew a long green line, named it "green", and proceeded to do a similar line named "red"; for some reason, he was now giggling and drew a further "black" line. His mother asked him what these lines represented and he first said they were "lamp-posts" and Mrs C recognised that he was

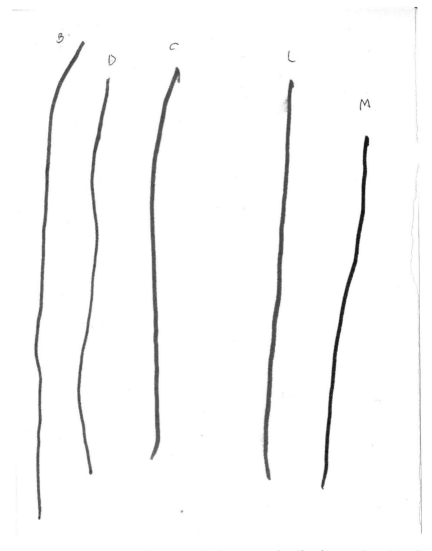

Figure 4. Claude's second drawing (Brafman—Dad—Claude—Louise—Mum).

having fun, teasing us with some game that was not being revealed. But then Claude declared that the "green" line was himself and the "red" line was Louise. We could not but join in the laughter, and Claude now added that "black" was his mother. Mrs C must have decided to defuse the growing excitement Claude was showing and moved back to her account of recent events. I had asked her to give us some information about herself and the family, which she was doing. But Claude continued with his game and, having drawn a "brown" line, he tried, in a determined way, to get his mother's attention, and then informed her that this line was his father. I thought I should help myself here and asked permission to put initials on each line, to remind myself of whom they represented. Claude was quite happy that I do this and, when I finished, he promptly did a further "brown" line and said that this was me. Mrs C told him my name and he found it quite hilarious, repeating it with ample laughter.

I thought I could recognise the theme of Claude's lines, since he had so clearly separated the males from the females, whilst making them all look exactly the same as each other. But my problem now was to discover some way of helping Claude to clarify what was behind those straight lines.

While Claude was making his drawing, Mrs C described her husband and herself as "media artists", and added that Mr C was away for quite long periods. "Oh", I said, "then he is a successful artist!" "Well", she answered, "an artist who works a lot ..." and we both laughed—she in amusement, and I rather apologetically for my *faux pas*. Mr C was much older than his wife, having children from his first marriage. Mrs C stopped work when her daughter was born. Louise was now just over five years old and attended a local primary school, where she was doing very well. Claude was now due to start at that school's nursery and the teachers had accepted quite well the fact of his still being in nappies. We discussed family routines and I learnt that the family had an easy-going attitude over baths and the use of toilets, so that the children had always been free to go there when either parent was having a bath or using the toilet. Claude was noticeably more interested than his sister was in watching his parents during these activities, though when it came to his urinating, whatever stratagems the parents used to persuade him to use the toilet, he managed to hold his urine until he had the nappy put on him. Mrs C gave me many examples of these episodes, where all participants had gone through endless arguments, promises, and tears, but eventually found that they had to give in to Claude's pleas.

It seemed Mrs C had adjusted very well to her husband's style of life and she had succeeded in building close, warm relationships with his children. She was a kind, caring mother, and it was obvious that she was keen to help Claude, but she could only put into practice those techniques which friends, health visitors, and doctors had recommended—all of which overlooked whatever anxiety the boy was harbouring.

Trying to devise some way of getting Claude to comment on "boys" and "girls", I voiced my wish that he would draw these figures, but he clearly would be unable to achieve this, so I asked Mrs C if she could, perhaps, help me out. She smiled and said that she would be happy to oblige. Claude himself offered her some felt-tip pens, choosing a colour for each picture that he proceeded to "request" his mother to draw. Claude was dictating each detail and when, at one point, Mrs C commented that something was missing, I asked her not to do this, but, instead, only follow the boy's instructions. She indicated that this made sense (Figure 5):

Figure 5. Claude's third drawing.

1. Blue, Claude himself, a boy. First, he asked for "legs", and Mrs C asked whether these should be fat or thin? "Fat", he answered. Then followed the ears, mouth, eyes, nappies/pants (he called them "pants"), and Claude asked for "a napkin", which he explained was to be used for breakfast time. Mrs C was intrigued that he was not asking for arms or a tummy or the shape of the head, but Claude had already given her the grey pen, asking her to draw "Mummy".
2. "Mummy" was even more incomplete than the first "boy", but fortunately Mrs C did not comment or make suggestions.
3. This was "Daddy", drawn in red—again, with no arms and with the angular-shaped napkin.
4. I cannot remember whether I or Mrs C asked Claude how he would draw "a girl": no arms again, but the same long hair as "Mummy", though this one had a body and a circular napkin.

I asked Mrs C for comments on the drawings. She was puzzled by the missing parts of the various bodies, but she added that, probably, Claude might not be able to explain the rationale for his unusual way of depicting the various members of the family. Claude was quietly following this conversation; he seemed pleased with his mother's drawing, but he was not volunteering any comments. I asked the psychologist for comments and, after a pause, she said that "one gets the impression that he has some conflict about the genital area". Mrs C was surprised at this comment, but as she concentrated, trying to figure out the plausibility of this idea, there was an expression of amusement in her eyes, as if she could see the logic of my colleague's opinion. And at this point, I took the plunge into the kind of translation that may appear extremely forceful, if not intrusive. I can only state, in mitigation, that this was one of those infrequent cases where one can feel most intensely that child and parent are totally aware of what is on show, even if they are unable to find the words to articulate their understanding. Of course, when addressing the family, I use language that the child can understand, but this is rather difficult to reproduce after the event, probably because, even as I put forward my ideas, I am constantly checking that the child is following my words and indicating some kind of understanding.

I said that the original straight lines showed that Claude can separate the sexes, but his fuller pictures depict them all as having no genitals; in fact, only Claude's drawing has a nappy/pants covering his genital area. Using the word familiar to Claude (supplied by Mrs C), I said that he seemed to be afraid that he would lose his "pee-pee", since he believed that his sister and his mother had lost theirs—hence the nappy, for protection. Claude had a vague grin on his face, but Mrs C was very thoughtful, finally saying: "I did wonder that he seemed to be more involved with us than with his father …".

I asked Claude how his father urinated and he promptly replied "standing up", so I suggested that maybe he would find it possible to pee in a standing position. Mrs C promptly said that she had tried that, many times, without success. But I now noticed that Claude was definitely holding his hand against his penis, and I suggested to Mrs C she might want to ask him what he thought of all that I had been saying. She did ask him and, to the surprise of all of us, he said that his "pee-pee has already been taken away". I asked him if this was in fact so, but, rather embarrassed, he replied that it was there. I could only surmise that he believed he had already lost part of his penis, being then afraid that he might lose what was left of it.

We had run out of time by this point, and I explained to Mrs C that Claude's anxiety was not that uncommon. I added that, seeing that his present crisis had been linked to his parents' absence on holiday, it was also possible that Claude might be dreading his starting at nursery school—that is, being away from them. Therefore, it might be useful if Mrs C would perhaps continue her attempts to get him to use the toilet and help him to understand that going to nursery and "peeing like his daddy" were both normal, positive steps in his growing up.

We had a second meeting one week later, when I was told that there was less anxiety and distress at home, but no change had occurred in Claude's behaviour. We discussed the various points that had emerged in our first meeting and arranged to meet again in two weeks' time. However, the meeting was cancelled and a new appointment was agreed upon. It turned out that this one was also cancelled, but this time I received a letter from Mrs C, in which she wrote:

> The toilet training has been a complete success. In the four weeks since our second meeting we had four accidents, all but one in bed and all but one in the first week. Since the beginning of the second week, we have been fine, including nights. We had a little trouble moving on to standing up to pee, but that is also sorted out now, as has his unwillingness to use toilets away from home. The last step will be to stop using the clip-on toilet seat, but I see no rush,

especially if that undermines his urge to be independent about his trips to the loo. I wanted to report our progress—there is obviously no need to have another appointment—and to thank you for your help. I am delighted the problem is behind us and that we got some insight into his difficulties, rather than just imposing socially acceptable behaviour over his worries.

Comments

Understandably, this letter has remained one of my most valued trophies and conclusive proof of the validity of my approach to these cases. Sadly, however, not all mothers are able to step back and reappraise what, in fact, determines their child's behaviour. Claude's "castration anxiety", to use the textbook diagnosis, is quite common among young boys and many of these are taken on for long-term psychotherapy. In fact, enuresis itself is the target of an enormous variety of therapeutic approaches. Most, if not all, of these techniques can claim success after some kind of interval. From a statistical point of view, it is possible to argue that the great majority of children will reach some eventual age when they achieve sphincter control. A strictly pragmatic view of the situation would show that the approach implemented depends entirely on the professional who is consulted. Urologists and surgeons will argue that each child should be "properly investigated", in case there is some underlying physical pathology, while some psychodynamically-oriented practitioners will stress the need for "proper emotional support" for the child. In between these extremes, there is no end of medicines, machines, technical stratagems, and kindly advice that parents are expected to adopt, and which the child has to endure.

Claude's case shows a very typical picture, where the child's presenting symptom is seen as abnormal behaviour requiring correction, but the parents' "corrective" behaviour is interpreted by the child as confirmation of his anxiety that some part of his body is abnormal or in danger of damage. At this point, distress escalates and very complex feelings invade all participants, most of which simply aggravate and reinforce the vicious circle between child and parents.

Understanding the nature of his anxiety helped Claude, but it is clear that his mother's totally different approach to him must have led him to realise that his sense of being under some danger no longer seemed justified. Once this vicious circle is broken, the way is open for child and parents to resume their normal functioning.

I wish all professionals would read the last sentence of Mrs C's letter and take her words into account when seeing their patients: *"I am delighted the problem is behind us and that we got some insight into his difficulties, rather than just imposing socially acceptable behaviour over his worries"*.

Wendy

The parents of this six-year-old girl came to consult me because she had been stealing things and masturbating compulsively "since the birth of her seven-month-old brother". I was told that this was a happy family, where the mother and father were engaged in successful and very active professional lives, but able parents who enjoyed caring for and spending time with their children. As they told me the family history I could not pick up any datum that might be significant to explain Wendy's recent behaviour.

Mrs W had suffered a miscarriage a couple of years after Wendy's birth and she found this very traumatic, but Wendy had shown no signs of being affected by her mother's distress or the atmosphere in the family home. It was only after the recent birth of her baby brother that Wendy began to show signs of distress. She had always enjoyed an active social life, having many friends in their neighbourhood and others who attended the same school. The Ws had a large family living not far from them and they often spent time together. Wendy had a close relationship with her grandparents. School reports consistently spoke very positively of Wendy's abilities and progress.

Wendy had recently told her mother that she wished she was a baby, which presumably indicated that she felt the baby had privileges that she envied. I was impressed by Mrs W's account of how she had dealt with Wendy's stealing: she had told her a couple of weeks earlier that "perhaps it is better that you talk to me about your feelings, rather than stealing things which can get you into trouble"—and Wendy stopped the stealing.

But the parents had not succeeded in helping Wendy to stop the masturbating. During our discussion they came to mention how Wendy and a cousin of hers had visited two brothers, friends of theirs, with whom they often had baths together. Coming home, Wendy had told her mother, in a tone of great pride, "I've also got a willy!" Mrs W tried to correct her and eventually asked Wendy to show her the "willy". She explained to Wendy that she had a clitoris—this was not a willy, which only boys have. Wendy was disappointed, but accepted her mother's explanation. However, the masturbation continued. The parents were puzzled and worried, but they were laughing at this account. I "allowed" myself to laugh and I told them that I believed that what they called "masturbation" was, in all probability, suggesting that this was Wendy's attempts to stretch her clitoris. They thought this was a funny idea.

The parents asked me how to proceed. I thought that if I asked to see Wendy the parents might interpret this as my not believing that they would be able to help the girl. I suggested, therefore, that they might explore Wendy's response to my translation of their account and, if this did not work, then to contact me again. Being a doctor, I thought I should also mention the advisability of ensuring she did not have some urinary tract or other infection.

Mrs W contacted me two weeks later to say that since seeing me and conveying my translation to Wendy, she had stopped her "masturbation". Some months later I heard from them that Wendy was making good progress and no further problems had appeared.

Comments

These parents are a perfect example of how a child's problems are influenced by the dynamics of the child–parents relationship. Mrs W had told me how she approached her daughter with questions and explanations, rather than with corrections, instructions, or punishment. Though surprised and amused by my interpretation of Wendy's behaviour, Mrs W was obviously prepared to put it to the test—and it seems that this was a correct reading of the girl's "masturbation", since her mother's words brought insight to Wendy and she was able to deal with her feelings in a different manner.

Dorothy

I saw Dorothy when she was six years old and, though our meeting helped her to overcome her presenting problem, she went on to experience a series of other difficulties. Sadly, her mother struggled with complex problems of her own and we never managed to offer effective long-term help to either of them.

Dorothy had individual sessions with a clinical psychologist over several months. For over one year, Dorothy had been constipated for periods of up to a fortnight. She had been admitted a few times to the paediatric ward of the local hospital, where appropriate intervention would lead to emptying of the bowels and a resumption of a more normal rhythm of defecation. However, as soon as Dorothy was discharged, the problems appeared again and readmission to hospital was required. The psychologist tried to teach Dorothy and her mother different techniques based on behavioural lines, but they invariably proved ineffective. Eventually, the psychologist decided to refer them to me, hoping they might respond to some insight-based approach.

Dorothy was a beautifully turned out six-year-old. She was shy and looked fearful when we first met, but she quickly relaxed and made herself at home. Mrs D was at ease from the moment we met, smiling in a warm, spontaneous way, as if we had known each other for a long time. No doubt, this would make it easier for Dorothy to relax, but only gradually did I discover that Mrs D's attitude of familiarity was also responsible for Dorothy's initial fearfulness. No sooner had I introduced myself to Dorothy and explained the kind of work I practised, she declared that she had already overcome her problems and she was sure I would confirm that she did not need any further treatment.

The psychologist, who had accepted my invitation to join us for the consultation, asked Dorothy how had it come about that her problems were gone. Dorothy said she had been going to the toilet regularly and, anyway, she had been dreading coming to see me. Dorothy was intelligent enough to perceive that this might be misinterpreted, so she added that these feelings were not related to me personally, but they had to do with the fact that she hated hospitals and she wished I would dismiss her before long. We all smiled at her tactfulness and tried to reassure her that this visit would be different to all the others, since I would not do anything invasive or hurtful—I only wanted to talk. Dorothy seemed to accept this reassurance and visibly relaxed.

Dorothy told me about her school life. She had many friends and felt she was quite popular among them. Her teachers seemed to be fond of her. Dorothy spoke with some sadness about the number of times she had to miss school due to her visits and admissions to hospital, but because hospital, home, and school were all in the same neighbourhood, her friends kept in touch with her. She said that life at home was very happy and told me about her recently born sibling. The baby was four months old and Dorothy described her with tones of pleasure and admiration. Mrs D commented about how she had feared Dorothy might resent the birth of the baby, but in fact she was proving to be "very mature" and always happy to help.

I asked Mrs D about her own life. She came from a large family. Her oldest sibling had died from leukaemia, but the others were all healthy. Mrs D laughed when she told me of her problems with feeding. She had gone through periods of being obsessed with eating and this meant putting on a lot of weight, which then led her to endless consultations in search of medical help. She had done very well at school and described herself as a successful professional. Her husband had immigrated to England some years earlier. He was an only child and was clearly pleased to be away from his family of origin. The couple discovered a shared talent for business and they had created their own small enterprise, which gave sufficient profit for them to lead a comfortable life.

As usual in cases of children with bowel problems, I enquired about the parents' toilet routines. It turned out that both grandmothers believed that constipation constitutes a poisoning of the body. Not only this, but Mr D's mother took this belief to a dramatic conclusion: Mrs D mimicked the mother-in-law, telling us that "come 9 a.m., she would look at the watch and if he had not been to the toilet, he either had to produce stools immediately or else he was given an enema!" It would, therefore, not be surprising to be told that both Mr and Mrs D had no fixed routine about their bowel habits. But Mrs D now burst out laughing; she did not want to mock me or anybody else who believed in fixed times for anything, but she wanted us to know how delighted she and her husband were that there was no fixed, established time for anything at all in their home—this held for meal times, bedtime, and anything else.

Dorothy surprised us at this point, saying to her mother that she wished mother were available at breakfast time. She added that her father would go to the toilet before breakfast (no doubt was left as to what he did there) and this meant Dorothy staying on her own, while her mother was, presumably, still fast asleep. For the first time in our meeting, Mrs D seemed rather embarrassed, not having expected to be shown up like this.

Dorothy had mentioned how painful defecation was and I asked how the parents dealt with her attempts to use the toilet. I was told that Mr D would insist that Dorothy should carry on trying, but Mrs D admitted that she could not cope with this and she would often interfere and plead on Dorothy's behalf, asking her husband to let her go. We tried to imagine how this dialogue unfolded, and we had serious misgivings about the atmosphere that was bound to develop over these situations. But Mrs D offered a rationale for her brand of protectiveness of Dorothy: "I thought the poor girl must be having the kind of pains one has in childbirth!" We were left to wonder what Dorothy made of this supposedly reassuring and comforting remark. Considering how recently the baby had been born, labour pains must have been a topical subject. Mrs D added that her family doctor was sure that Dorothy's problems were linked to the baby's birth, but Mrs D argued that she had complained of the constipation much earlier than the pregnancy, and added that Dorothy could not possibly know anything of what went on during labour, since she had only heard about the pain after the event.

Several times during Mrs D's account I wanted to stop at some detail for more detailed enquiry, but I was worried that, once started, Mrs D would not manage to stop. It was towards the end of the interview that I heard confirmation of what my intuition was warning me: Mrs D simply loved talking to doctors. As an outpatient, as much as an inpatient, Mrs D was very attached, if not plainly dependent, on a doctor's support. And this attachment could be gratified by consultations about herself as much as when discussing Dorothy's problems. Learning this particular aspect of Mrs D's relationship with doctors and hospitals made me understand why Dorothy was so afraid of hospitals— I believe she had sensed how important it was for her mother to gain contact with doctors, even if through Dorothy's symptoms. On another level, it seemed very likely that Mrs D could not recognise Dorothy's personal experience of her difficulties.

I tried to discuss the actual events surrounding defecation. Dorothy found this somewhat difficult, but Mrs D helped to fill in the picture; gradually, we recognised that Dorothy was able to register her body urges and she knew that she should go to the toilet. She could make her way there, but then she stopped: she took her pants down and then found that she could not make herself actually sit on the toilet. I did not expect her to be able to express in words what exactly frightened her about that particular step in the sequence, so I asked Dorothy if she could perhaps make some drawing.

She drew (Figure 6) a "Ninja turtle" ("like the one I have here on my watch", she explained) underground, under the street level, near a manhole.

The line in the middle of the road showed how the scene was being observed from outside, and the pavement line clarified this further. The sky was quite empty, but she later coloured it in. She did not pause for long and drew a second picture (Figure 7): this now showed "how it is inside", with water running and dripping all round, all very dark and scary. I thought that the size of the manhole gave a likely idea of the intensity of Dorothy's anxiety.

I could understand the content of Dorothy's unconscious fantasy, but this is the point where it is difficult to decide how much to interpret to the child. The fact that she put a creature "inside" would strongly suggest fantasies related to pregnancy, much as the degree of magnification of the manhole might point to further ideas about a baby's growth. I decided to restrict myself to a vaguer statement of her anxiety

Figure 6. Dorothy's first drawing.

Figure 7. Dorothy's second drawing.

and I said that the pictures showed how very different things are when they are seen from outside or when from inside: in the first picture, people would think there is a small hole and they would know nothing of what happens inside, but the second picture showed how things inside are huge, dark, wet, and scary. I added that this was probably why she was so afraid of sitting on the toilet, because she did not know what exactly would come out. Dorothy nodded her head, confirming that this made sense to her.

Mrs D was fascinated by my comments. She asked Dorothy whether I was right and Dorothy confirmed I was. We discussed how to proceed and I went through the routine of urging Mrs D to institute some sort of fixed time for Dorothy to sit on the toilet, but I had little hope that she would manage to do this.

Follow-up appointments were missed, but Mrs D told the clinic secretary that Dorothy was managing to sit on the toilet and defecate. According to my paediatric colleagues, Dorothy was not brought back again because of being constipated, but appointments continued to be made for a wide range of reasons. The maximal shock for me was to learn a couple of years later that Mrs D had requested a surgical ligature of her jaws, as a last resort to stop herself from over-eating. Certainly the issue of control over intake and output was a central feature in the life of Mrs D—and, at least for some years, of Dorothy.

Comments

Dorothy left me with a profound sense of sadness and hopelessness. The development of Dorothy's body functions and body image was so intimately linked to her mother's pathology that it would be difficult not to be pessimistic about Dorothy's future. When I saw her, reports suggested that she was managing to keep her academic, social, and intellectual development independent from her parents' influence, but for how long would she manage to do this?

Mrs D was offered regular counselling or therapy, which she turned down. We tried to get Dorothy into individual psychotherapy, but this never got off the ground. Apparently, the only positive datum that can be reported is Dorothy's capacity to convey her unconscious anxieties through her drawings and, luckily, the subsequent success in gaining control of her bowel functioning. Credit must be given to Mrs D's capacity to help her daughter overcome this problem.

Jane*

Jane's story is a rich illustration of the ways in which a child will use physical complaints to convey distress to his or her parents. Jane's case presents important evidence to show that the physical symptoms have come to constitute, first and foremost, a language learnt from the interaction with the parent(s). The child will "learn" which language his parents can grasp and respond to—if a parent only reacts to physical complaints, these will multiply. Indeed, the particular choice of organ and problem will have a specific meaning for the child and, therefore, this should be looked into, but we must not lose sight of the purpose served by the symptom within the child's relationship to the parent(s).

Jane was a very intelligent and articulate eight-year-old who attended a highly academic school, where she always achieved good results. She was a shy and sensitive girl, but she had many friends and all of her teachers were fond of her. One day, she began to complain of troublesome headaches and this led to her being "placed somewhere quiet until she felt better". The general practitioner was consulted after this had gone on for about four months. In his letter to the paediatrician, he

---

*Previously published in *Untying the Knot* (Brafman, 2001).

mentioned that Jane now also complained of "a curious sensation in the head that appears about once each week and lasts for a few minutes each time". This was "a sensation of a shower of rain or light passing up through her head and during this time she is unable to concentrate and needs to sit quietly". The GP had found no abnormality in his examination, but he wondered whether Jane might be presenting "a migrainous condition or even some sort of curious epileptiform phenomenon".

Jane had a skull x-ray and an electroencephalogram; both produced normal results. The paediatrician explored in depth Jane's account of her symptoms, and she also learnt of recent family events that had affected Jane's life. Her conclusion was that she could find no evidence of organic pathology and, while being prepared to request ophthalmological and neurological assessments, she felt that a psychiatric evaluation should be undertaken first. Fortunately, Jane's mother agreed to this and they were referred to me.

Jane and Mrs J formed a very attractive pair. Mrs J was young, good looking, well dressed, and self-possessed; Jane was pretty and immaculately turned out, though shy and reserved. Jane was able to tell me about her symptoms, particularly her "funny feelings"; she provided detailed descriptions of noises, lights, and mainly water coming up her head whenever she looks into slits, holes, or at certain illuminated surfaces.

The doctors had described these symptoms in their reports, and both Jane and her mother had obviously gone through these many times before. Jane spoke calmly, but there was no doubt that she was frightened by her experiences, and Mrs J's comments indicated a fear about what illness might be causing them. I asked Jane about life at home and school and I soon found myself thoroughly confused by all the names and relationships. Jane and her mother were quite used to such a reaction and they laughed warmly about my muddle, promptly setting out to help me to understand the complexity of their family structure. Jane's father had left the family when she was very little. He lived "around the corner" and kept in close contact with Jane, her brother, and their mother. He had remarried three years previously and his wife had given birth to a baby not too long ago. Mrs J had also remarried recently and her new husband had children from a previous marriage.

Mrs J told me that her new husband had been involved with the family for a long time before they actually married. But I noticed that Jane dated this marriage as "four months ago", a date which matched the time when her symptoms had first appeared. It was striking that both male and female members of the family network were eminently successful people in their chosen fields of work. Mrs J herself worked as a high-powered administrator, and over the years she had achieved considerable success in the various areas to which she had turned. She had an impressive command of language and, judging by how easily she made herself comfortable when talking to me, she was clearly very able to make contact with people.

As Jane was telling me about her daily life and the transition from home to school environments, she suddenly mentioned, quite in passing, that she was enuretic. I was taken by surprise, since there had been no reference to this in the correspondence I had received. It was not just the question of Jane's age, but she was clearly a girl who took great pride in her physical appearance and I could only imagine that she would feel deeply ashamed about wetting her bed. But I was even more surprised by Mrs J's reaction to her daughter's revelation: at first, she just laughed, but then she put into words the fact that she could not see why I attached any importance to Jane's bedwetting.

It would be difficult to reconstruct the discussion that followed. Jane must have known that her mother's views about the significance of the wetting were different to her own. Her embarrassment was acute; she was visibly struggling, caught between her wish to tell me about the wetting and the obvious awareness of her mother's incapacity to accept her account of her feelings—at least, about this particular experience.

Mrs J tried to put the record straight by telling me that "as a matter of fact Jane has not wet her bed in a long time". Jane meekly stated that she had done so even the previous night. Mrs J was astonished and it was some time before they sorted out how it was that both of them were correct in their statements. It emerged that the morning starts for Jane with her nanny coming into the room (I had not known there was such a person in the house), and Jane reported how, if it happens that she has wet her bed during the night, she will say a plaintive "sorry" to the nanny. It is the nanny who takes charge of changing the bedclothes and Jane is acutely aware of her fear that the nanny will report the wetting to her mother. But before the nanny's appearance, Jane has already gone through a private ordeal. She described with obvious shame how she wakes up as soon as she wets herself; she gets out of bed and goes to the bathroom, where she undresses, washes, and dries herself, before returning to bed, where she puts the towel between herself and the sheet.

But the family followed a routine that explained how Jane and her mother managed to hold on to the stories that each of them had created.

Whatever happens in the night, when Jane wakes up and gets washed and ready for the day, she gets dressed and then goes to the kitchen, where she makes a cup of tea that she lovingly takes to her mother in bed—so, from Mrs J's point of view, there had been no wetting in a long time. Mrs J was very upset when she heard Jane's account.

But no sooner was the incidence of the wetting sorted out, I found that a new disagreement/misunderstanding developed about its significance. Mrs J told us that when she had spoken to her own mother about Jane's wetting, she had reminded Mrs J that she had wet her bed until she was ten years old. She was laughing when recounting this and I indicated my puzzlement. I asked her if she had any memories about the wetting itself or whether this was something she was prepared to accept as a correct story from her mother. She said that she did not have clear memories about the event or how often it happened, but she did remember quite vividly experiencing a feeling of pleasure: "The wet enveloping you, so very nice—true, the next morning it felt awful, but …".

Jane burst out with an uncontrolled "It is *horrid*!" that surprised both me and Mrs J. The way in which Mrs J went on speaking about Jane's reaction made me think that, somehow, Mrs J had taken her expression of violent objection to represent Jane's agreement with her views—that is, that the "horridness" lay in the wetting becoming known to others. I looked at Jane and asked her if I had understood her mother correctly and whether this interpretation was correct. She hesitated before muttering a "yes", confirming that she agreed with her mother. I said I was surprised because I felt that Jane's account of how disturbed she was by the wetting and how she dealt with this during the night would suggest that it was the experience of wetting herself and lying in the wet clothes that produced strong feelings in her. Mrs J promptly indicated her disagreement with my interpretation and turned to Jane, asking her to tell us what she thought of what I had said. Jane lowered her head and obviously struggled before she managed to say, quietly, "he is right".

Both Jane and her mother were disturbed by this unexpected sequence and the appearance of a conflict where Jane's loyalty was put to the test. I tried to explain the reason for my pursuing what I had thought was a disagreement: it was quite natural for Mrs J to interpret Jane's reaction to the wetting along the lines of what had been her own experience, but unless Jane managed to make her mother aware of what she herself went through, Mrs J could not but conclude that her understanding was correct—and Jane would remain under the belief that her mother expected her to profess agreement with this reading of her emotional experience, even though it did not, in fact, match her own feelings about it. I did not expand on the implications of this overt compliance, though, from what I had been told about Jane's life in her extended family, it seemed to be an important factor in Jane's attitude toward the adults around her.

At this point, I suggested that Jane made a drawing. I was hoping that this might give us further insight into Jane's feelings and I would also have the opportunity of talking to Mrs J about the environment in which Jane had grown up. Indeed, Mrs J was quite happy to explain in more detail the many changes that had characterised Jane's home life. Formal relationships had been formed and dissolved, but Mrs J seemed quite sure that a good atmosphere had always prevailed and that all the adults had consistently sustained not just civilized attitudes to each other, but also friendly and supportive ones. I wondered whether she could imagine that Jane harboured feelings of unhappiness or disappointment, but this was a hypothesis that she would never consider, in practice, possible.

I do not think it is necessary to repeat here all the information I obtained from Mrs J, as it is not really relevant to understand what followed. I had noticed that Jane had started to draw something, but then turned the page round before drawing the picture that she eventually showed us. She said that "the tree had gone wrong" and she had, therefore, started the picture again.

On the left of the tree (Figure 8), a mother and daughter are standing together.

Their arms are raised "because that is how I like to draw people". An aunt is on the other side, holding a basket where a bird is going to fall; the radio is switched on and there is noise coming out of it. I asked why the bird was falling and what would happen to it, but Jane explained that she did not know why this was so. "Wee" is the rendering of the noise of the bird falling. Mrs J thought she should pre-empt any Freudian extrapolations and explained that the family word for urine is "pee", not "wee". Unexpectedly, Mrs J said that the tree in the picture looked like the one they have in their garden and Jane confirmed this, clearly pleased that her mother had identified that element of her drawing.

Looking more carefully at the picture, I noticed that the little girl's hand is very near a stain between the mother's legs, but I decided not

Figure 8. Jane's first drawing.

to mention this. I also wondered if there was a connection between the raised hands and a denial of contact between hands and genitals, but again I left this unspoken. Instead, I called their attention to my impression that the bird would fall not into the basket, but rather hit the aunt on the head. Jane burst out laughing, quite amused at this idea. Mrs J attempted a smile, but I thought she had now become rather impatient with what interpretations I put on my "discoveries".

In fact, I did not enlarge on my comment. We had now been together for over ninety minutes and I thought we should bring the interview to a close. I offered them a second meeting and tried to make explicit a couple of points from our discussion. I suggested that Jane kept a record of significant events in the following two weeks, when we would meet again, so that we could explore any possible correlation with her wetting. I mentioned, as if in passing, that there might be some connection between the "water coming up the head" and the problem of wetting, but I mostly stressed that I believed that her symptoms were her way of trying to convey her feelings to her mother—and unless she found a way of articulating these feelings clearly, her mother would remain unable to understand her. I did not put into words the corresponding need for her mother to be prepared to *listen* to what Jane might want to say, but I hoped that Mrs J was able to infer this from the course of the interview.

When I met Jane and her mother two weeks later, they were pleased to report that Jane had not wet her bed since our interview. Jane was clearly proud of this. Mrs J had picked up my cue and she had spent considerable time speaking to Jane and trying to learn of her feelings—but, very much in passing, I was told of a development that I could never guess was possible.

As we were talking, Jane had picked up some sheets of paper and she was drawing two girls (Figure 9): one wearing glasses and the other not.

Figure 9. Jane's second drawing.

Jane commented that she wanted to use glasses and added that her brother wants to use braces. Mrs J laughed, saying that "they obviously think this is fashionable". She went on to tell me that she had taken Jane to an ophthalmologist. I assumed this was a long-standing appointment and Jane's remark probably meant that some glasses had been prescribed. I was not prepared, therefore, for Mrs J telling me why she had decided to have Jane's eyes tested: when I pointed out during our first meeting that the bird in Jane's picture would fall on the woman's head, rather than fall in the basket as Jane had meant to depict the scene. Mrs J remembered that Jane occasionally has trouble in reading her music and she concluded that there must be something wrong with her sight.

Jane explained that the girl without glasses does not want to have any, whilst the other one likes to have them: "no, actually she does not want them ... but does not mind them". I found it quite painful to see Jane using her picture to indicate her own efforts to present a façade of acceptance of something she clearly did not like or want to have to do—whilst her mother could not see any connection between the comments on the drawing and Jane's own feelings. Mrs J made it quite plain that she thought Jane was simply telling me the story of two girls in a picture.

I put into words my impression that Jane seemed to find it very difficult to voice any feelings of opposition against what she takes as the adults' expectations of her. I asked Jane if she could imagine herself actually saying "no, I do not want". She lifted her shoulders, bowed her head, and muttered "not really". Mrs J said that there were many times when it was quite impossible to get Jane to do something she felt it was important for her to do. I thought that if Jane saw herself as incapable of being openly defiant, even if this was no more than ordinary self-assertion, her mother was determined to describe her as self-confident and, at times, stubborn. I wondered that perhaps Mrs J thought I was trying to provoke Jane into conforming with my own idea of her and decided to let the matter rest, in case we ended up putting Jane into a situation where she might feel stuck in a conflict of loyalties.

We arranged a further appointment for three weeks later.

Our third meeting brought a mixture of good, positive developments and a sad warning that whatever progress we managed to make in our meetings might not be further built upon. Jane's difficulty in making open, explicit statements of her needs and wishes seemed to persist and she seemed to find in her symptoms the only "acceptable" language in which to convey her sense of disappointment or disillusionment. Mrs J, on the other hand, had made a determined effort to come closer to Jane, but she still retained an intense disbelief that this closeness might be in any way related to the progress made by Jane in overcoming her various symptoms.

Both Jane and her mother seemed in great spirits. The headaches and "funny feelings" had disappeared and she had coped extremely well with the last weeks of term at school. Jane had done very well in her exams and the teachers had commented that she appeared a much happier child. At home, the picture was similar and Mrs J was pleased with Jane's progress. A negative note was the fact that Jane had wet her bed three nights over the preceding week, an event that upset Jane, particularly as she could not understand why this symptom had recurred.

Mrs J was extremely proud of how much she had talked to Jane. She felt this was a remarkable discovery, the more surprising when she had never been aware of keeping any distance between herself and her much-loved daughter. She recounted with pleasure how she had reported her "discovery" to many members of the family, with all the pride that goes with a newfound skill. Against this background, it was disconcerting to hear Mrs J saying that Jane had probably wet her bed because her brother had come back from boarding school or—"who knows?"—it might have been due to the fact that her school term had come to an end and since she was now going to sleep later than usual, this might lead to her sleeping far too deep and not noticing when she wanted to pee.

Jane told me about her plans for the holidays. She was to spend some time with grandmother and then stay with her father abroad, after which she would join her mother for the last stretch of the holiday. Without any warning, she began to cry. No sobs or visible movements, just sad, silent tears that rolled down her cheeks, whilst Jane looked immensely helpless. I indicated my surprise and Mrs J offered words of sympathy, but Jane was at a loss to explain why she was crying at this point.

As the silence persisted, I suggested that Jane should make a drawing, whilst I continued speaking to her mother. I was hoping that her picture(s) might help us to understand the reason for her tears.

Jane concentrated in her drawing, though it was clear that she was following my conversation with her mother. I find it difficult to reproduce the nuances of the dialogue that followed. This was a sensitive, loving, extremely articulate young woman, whose life—and especially her work—must have brought her into contact with innumerable people in distress. She was living in an age where it was just impossible not to read and to hear of the link between emotions and bodily symptoms—and yet, having just described Jane's progress and her own efforts to achieve this result, here was Mrs J putting forward hypotheses that failed to take this into account. I have quoted above two of these, but as our conversation moved on and we considered again how the wetting had stopped, Mrs J commented: "I suppose it was some physical failure that came right, after all ...".

This was not the first time I found this puzzling attitude of disbelief regarding a child overcoming her bedwetting. Mrs J's interpretation of Jane's improvement indicated her doubt that this was a permanent achievement. This is only too commonly found with a parent who struggled with a sphincter dysfunction in her own childhood. She starts off by assuming that the child's symptom is "the same thing" that she had in her childhood, which leads her to expect that the child will only overcome it at the same point as she got rid of her problem. However, these parents invariably convey a sense that they had nothing to do with the cessation of their dysfunction. Each person weaves their own rationalisation to explain why the wetting (or the messing) disappeared one day, but the underlying layer is one of total helplessness—pain, distress, and shame while the symptom persisted, and relief once it disappeared. Sadly, when seen as adults, they will seldom admit to these sentiments; instead, they recount various face-saving manoeuvres they used so as to disguise the problem, but these hardly hide the experience of being saved by a miracle and then living for a long time under the fear that the symptom might return.

When their child overcomes the sphincter dysfunction following a therapeutic intervention, these parents can feel very disturbed. One of the parents I saw kept repeating, with great anguish, the accusation that her mother had not sought "the right help". And when a child improves, as Jane did, thanks to a parent understanding the child's need for a closer emotional contact, there is the danger that this parent feels guilty for not having spotted earlier what these needs were.

I felt that Mrs J was struggling with feelings like these. She must have sensed that Jane was using her physical symptoms to bring about some closeness with her, but her need to sort out her feelings about her own past and for her earlier approach to Jane probably made it impossible for her to abandon her views that the wetting, the headaches, and all the "funny feelings" had some organic underlying cause.

Jane indicated that she had finished her drawing (Figure 10) and I asked her to describe it to us.

The sun and clouds are drawn in yellow. Under the water, a fish is going to eat a tadpole that is running away and then proceeds to eat the other tadpole that is eating some reeds; some frogspawn float further away. Jane did not know why she had drawn this scene and she shrugged her shoulders, in silence, at several questions we put to her. Mrs J praised her warmly, saying it was "a very nice picture".

I decided to ignore who was eating whom or what projections were depicted in this "destructive", "oral sadistic" scene. Instead, I voiced my impression that it might be significant that the light and beauty prevailing above water gave no clue to what was going on underneath. Mrs J burst out laughing, perhaps more kindly than friendly: "Oh, come! That is all to do with what they have learnt at school".

Figure 10. Jane's third drawing.

I decided to try again with my reading of the picture and said that "I believe the picture might be a reflection of what Jane feels and the explanation for her crying: she may find it difficult to keep bright and sunny, while keeping to herself all the turmoil underneath". Mrs J turned to Jane and asked "do you think he is right?" and Jane nodded, again crying in silence. Mrs J was dumbfounded.

I thought I should make some connection between this sense of failed communication and the previous efforts that had brought them together. "I do not pretend to know what exactly *caused* the wetting, but I do believe it stopped because you [addressing Mrs J] came closer to Jane, as you described. It may well be that your telling the family about it made Jane fear that you might feel you had talked enough. Plus the coming holidays, where apparently Jane will spend long periods with other relations, may have heightened her fear of losing you again." Mrs J could not see much sense in this, but she turned to Jane and said "could that really be so?", and, again, Jane nodded her head.

It was clear that it would be some time before we met again, if at all. I carefully pointed out to Mrs J that, however gratifying it was to see Jane get rid of her physical symptoms, I felt they should bear in mind the possibility of her having some individual psychotherapy at a later point. Jane was clearly a very sensitive child and she might need further help to improve her self-confidence. Mrs J barely disguised her reluctance in contemplating such a plan, but we left it that they would let me know how Jane was getting on after the holidays and the start of the new school term.

When I heard from Mrs J, she reported that "Jane seems to be much more relaxed than she was some months ago and she is certainly much more able to confide her worries to me". The bedwetting "is virtually non-existent" and if it happens that something brings on "the funny feeling" (she quoted the example of "a plate of fried, mashed potato slightly burnt at the edges"), Jane reports it "with an apologetic smile" and makes it clear that the sensation does not persist for any length of time. Mrs J added that Jane "still remains a sensitive little girl who cannot bear ever to be second-best at home or at school" and she went on to quote Jane's occasional reaction of distress at the possibility of being displaced by a sibling in her parents' love.

But Mrs J's letter conveyed very clearly her feeling that there was now a close relationship between Jane and herself that allowed her to help Jane whenever this was necessary. She assured me that she would take my advice if I felt that psychotherapy was still necessary, but I wrote back to confirm my support for the changes that she had implemented. I would be happy to see Jane again, but only if and when she and/or her mother wished me to do so.

Comments

My decision not to urge Mrs J to let Jane have psychotherapy was determined by my impression that such a recommendation might be seen by Mrs J as a statement of my doubt about her reliability as a helper. I must confess that I was, indeed, uncertain that Mrs J would sustain her attitude of interest and closeness with Jane, but on balance I decided to take a stance that might lead Mrs J to feel that I trusted her capacity to continue to help Jane.

I did obtain some follow-up information on Jane, but only over a few months. The GP told me that he had not been consulted further for symptoms similar to the original ones and I did not hear from the family again. My impression was that Jane would face considerable difficulties on reaching adolescence, since her difficulty with self-assertion and her basically unconfident self-image would point to a considerable need for external support. Even considering the extremely complex family arrangements around her, this might not prove to be enough to help her with her need for self-discovery.

I found Jane's a very painful case. Lack of parental support is usually associated with lack of sophistication, poverty, or serious personal conflicts in the parents that impede them from recognising the child's needs. None of these were present in Jane's life. Mrs J was genuinely caring and willing to help her, but her attitude to "feelings" appeared to lead her to a serious blindness regarding Jane's emotional experiences. It is possible that Mrs J had personal problems that were not identified, but from our meetings I thought that Mrs J was not prepared to look at Jane's problems as anything other than physical events. I was puzzled by her apparent belief that Jane's need for closeness could be satisfied by any adult who happened to make themselves available.

Leon

The paediatrician saw Leon when he was seven-and-a-half years old. For the previous year, Leon had been messing himself, though he had been in full control of his sphincters before that. The consultant was told that Leon was able to defecate in the toilet once or twice per week, after which his soiling improved for a few days. Physical examination did not reveal any significant abnormality and the consultant prescribed a small dose of laxatives. He discussed the general situation and urged the parents to make Leon go regularly to the toilet, to help his body to develop a regular rhythm.

When the consultant paediatrician saw Leon one month later, he was told that there had been no change in the situation. He did not feel justified in embarking on complex gastrointestinal investigations, but at the same time, he had been unable to elicit any history of events that might have represented a traumatic experience for the boy. On balance, he suggested to the parents that, before having further tests, it might be helpful to refer Leon for a child psychiatric assessment. Mr and Mrs L decided they had nothing to lose by trying out this unexpected recommendation.

Leon and his parents came to see me, and before long we had an atmosphere that could only be described as merry. Leon was a delightful, intelligent boy who was very aware of his problem and made it clear that he was eager to find anything that would release him from a symptom that made him feel helpless and ashamed. Mr and Mrs L clearly enjoyed a joke and they seemed proud of their light-hearted way of facing life and people in general. They accepted my request that they should allow Leon to answer my questions and they laughed at Leon's answers, though from time to time they would make some funny comment about his stories.

Leon told me about his school life. He was making good progress from an academic point of view and he had a wide circle of friends, both at school and in his neighbourhood. His peers did not know of the soiling, since this occurred mostly at home; there had been times he messed himself when playing with friends outside the house, but he had managed to run home before his friends discovered it. He had a younger sister and he told me of their relationship, which seemed quite unremarkable. After we talked for some time, I asked Leon to make some drawings, while I asked his parents for further information. He was happy to do this and soon was concentrating on his drawing, though he followed closely our conversation and occasionally put in a funny comment on what his parents were telling me.

Mr and Mrs L accepted my request to tell me something about their backgrounds; they could understand that knowing about the two of them, and also about the development of the family, would give me a clearer background against which to place Leon's difficulties.

Mrs L was the youngest of thirteen children and from a very young age was cast in the role of caretaker of her ageing mother. This had led to rather irregular school attendance and Mrs L had never been able to make up for the formal learning she had missed out on. She told me, in a self-deprecating tone of voice, that she still struggled with the written word—and, at this point, Mr L interjected that this was one problem they both shared. Whatever I might imagine they would feel about such an impediment, I had to accept that, for them, this appeared to be just one more of those facts of life that one has to learn to live with. Mrs L was proud of her marriage and she claimed to be content with her life, looking after her family and keeping in touch with her extended family.

Mr L was the second of six children. He had grown up among much violence, with frequent rows between the parents and the children being disciplined through shouts and brute force. He recounted with much laughter that he had wet himself until the age of seven, when one day his father ran after him with a burning piece of paper, threatening to burn him unless he stopped wetting himself. Mr L turned to his wife and, still laughing, asked her "and I never did it again, did I?" She was obviously used to this brand of humour and replied, laughing lovingly "never, not once, darling". Mr L had worked in many different jobs and for some time now he was working for his wife's brother, an experience that, in spite of his jokes, sounded as if it was quite disastrous.

Predictably, the family had an easy-going style of life, where strictness or discipline were virtually non-existent. At several points during our meeting they started discussions to establish how best to answer some question of mine and soon they would end up laughing, clearly unable to reach a compromise. This occurred, for example, when they wanted to tell me about somebody's age or about the date for some particular event. Meal-times, ordinary household events—all seemed to take place according to factors that were never predetermined, so that the word "routine" had no application in their daily life. Leaving apart this aspect of family life, there was no doubt that this was a well-integrated, close, warm, happy family.

Leon's soiling had started about eighteen to twenty-four months earlier; the parents were unable to agree on a precise timing. They did, however, manage to agree that the soiling had started not long after Leon had an operation for a squint. He had recovered well from the operation, but he soon developed a pattern of messing, where he would pass a motion about once each week, followed by an improvement in the soiling; but gradually the soiling again increased, irrespective of diets, medication, and many stratagems that the parents had put into practice.

When we were discussing the soiling, it emerged that Leon's younger sister had also had a brief episode of messing at the time when Leon's encopresis started. Very much in passing, Mr and Mrs L told me that Mrs L's mother had died not long before the children developed these symptoms. We got quite confused when trying to establish the chronological sequence of these events, and at one point the parents were convinced that not much time had passed between these various events I was focusing on, and yet repeatedly they would quote the same "two years ago" or "about one year before" to refer to them. Whatever the real sequence, they insisted that the grandmother's death occurred well before Leon's messing. What surprised me was the unexpected reference to a detail of the circumstances of this grandmother's final illness: she had died after a stroke, but this had first manifested itself by her developing a sudden squint. The parents reported the anxiety that had been created in the family by the "slow bleeding in the brain" that had "killed her in one week", but it was obvious that they had never considered that Leon might have made a conscious or unconscious link between his own squint operation and the significance of the same phenomenon in his grandmother's final illness.

When Leon began to soil himself, Mr L had reacted quite angrily to his messing and I was told that he had even hit Leon a few times. For her part, Mrs L had resorted to many different ways of dealing with Leon: she had tried to reassure him, just as often as she had criticised him or, at other times, pretended to ignore what was happening. They had consulted the general practitioner and had followed advice given by friends and professionals, but they had not found any measures that produced effective results.

I now turned to Leon's drawings, which he described to us. His first drawing (Figure 11) was a rather crude stork. He could not explain why he had drawn this, only saying that he knew it was "an African bird".

He had next drawn a "Union Jack" (Figure 12), but he had "got the colours wrong". The third picture (Figure 13) showed a "cowboy" and he told us a long and complicated story about this. His voice became animated as he told us that the cowboy was wearing two trousers and he was shot at by "a little man" (he drew red blobs to mark the places hit by the shots), and four of these had hit "the stomach"; the cowboy had shot himself in the left arm and Leon said that the little man's eighth shot would kill the cowboy. He now drew a snake (Figure 14), using the same black and red pens he had used for the cowboy, but he could not explain why he had drawn each half of the snake with each of these colours.

I thought that Leon's fifth drawing (Figure 15) had a different quality, compared to the previous ones. He had depicted "a flying fish", and this was surrounded by lines—these could either represent waves in the water or else act as disguises to keep the fish hidden from sight. When I asked Leon several questions about this drawing, he seemed rather embarrassed. He laughed, trying to find answers, but these seemed clearly improvised, rather than thoughts that had already been available to him when he originally drew the fish. He told me that he had drawn "a frame" around the fish and said that this was "a picture" and not just an illustration of a fish inside a fish-tank.

Figure 11. Leon's first drawing.

Leon now picked up another sheet of paper and drew a frame (Figure 16), inside which he drew a multitude of lines, saying that it was a maze. He could not explain the blue triangles, but he wrote "in" and "out" to mark the entrance and exit. The parents were making

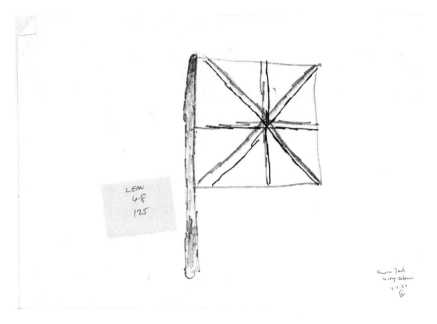

Figure 12. Leon's second drawing.

occasional comments about my conversation with Leon and at this point they mentioned that, for some inexplicable reason, Leon refuses to eat solids when he joins the family for the evening meal. I noticed that Leon wrote the "in" sign at the same time that Mr and Mrs L told me of this food habit.

When I thought it was clear that Leon had finished his drawings, I invited him and his parents to go through all the pictures he had made. I asked what they made of these; Leon did not add anything and his parents restricted their comments to some adjectives about the quality of the drawings. I offered to describe what I thought was a story that was depicted in the pictures. I said nothing about Leon's spellings, but I told him that I suspected the stork might have something to do with stories about how babies are born. The pictures of the flag perhaps indicated his feeling that there was something wrong, not just in the drawing but also somewhere else. The cowboy struck me as bringing into sharp focus a person's belly, with four shots hitting it. The snake appeared to illustrate some division of a unit into two, though I could not say exactly what this referred to. The fish looked to me like Leon's idea of a baby inside its mother's body. Finally, the maze seemed to

Figure 13. Leon's third drawing.

depict a very confused idea of the insides of a body—now no longer a mother's body but any person's—and I suggested that perhaps this was a representation of what Leon thought was the inside of his own body—that is, he can recognise a place for things to go in and another

Figure 14. Leon's fourth drawing.

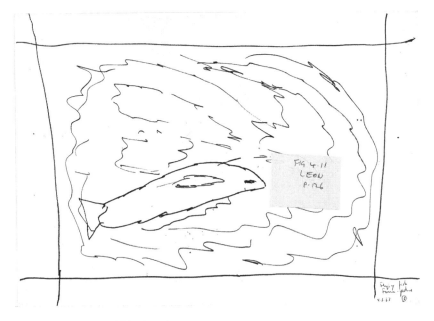

Figure 15. Leon's fifth drawing.

Figure 16. Leon's sixth drawing.

place for them to come out, but he was confused about what goes on inside it and perhaps the same confusion existed about what might come out of it.

Leon smiled, with a faint touch of recognition of something familiar. Mr and Mrs L laughed, clearly amused at what I was saying, but then Mrs L remembered that two days earlier (at which point Mr L corrected her, saying it had been three days earlier), Leon had asked her if it was true that babies were born through the underneath of the body. She answered that "yes, that was true". Leon had firmly replied that he did not believe her, since one of his friends at school had told him that babies came out of the mothers through "the front". Both parents discussed the question of schoolchildren and the problems that result from their exchange of stories, but Leon looked as if he had worked something out. He was looking at me and I repeated my previous interpretation, but now in different words, saying that Leon obviously *knew* some facts about the body, but that he still seemed to *feel* muddled about the possibility that digestion and pregnancy might take place in the same organs.

I now discussed with Mr and Mrs L the importance of helping Leon to develop a routine for his bowels to open every day at the same time; I suggested they should get him to sit on the toilet each morning and evening, always at the same time. The parents were to make a chart and Leon would get two points for each day in which he defecated normally, without messing himself. We arranged another appointment for two weeks later, and it was agreed that if Leon reached twenty-eight points, his father would give him an "Action Man" figure of Leon's choice.

When Leon came back with his parents two weeks later, he was beaming and showing off the "Action Man" he had been given. Mr and Mrs L showed me the chart, where it was obvious that Leon had scored two points every day of the previous fortnight. The rest of the meeting had the feeling of some celebration. Leon was relieved and proud, clearly confident that he had overcome his problem. Mr and Mrs L were prepared to give some value to their managing to institute some definite routine in their child's life, but they remained incredulous that my translation of Leon's anxieties might have played a significant role in the sequence of events. They certainly seemed to believe that Leon had "turned a corner" and would now take responsibility for his bowel movements.

The family contacted me again two weeks later to say that Leon continued to have effective visits to the toilet every day. We left it that they would get in touch at a later date, if this proved necessary. Some months later I asked the paediatrician and the general practitioner for news on Leon and as neither had heard from the family again, we had to assume that Leon was doing well.

Comments

It is possible to consider the hypothesis that Leon's problems over the control of his body's contents was linked to comments he heard regarding his grandmother's final illness after developing a squint. But though this was mentioned in our meeting, no explicit link was suggested. Leon's unconscious fantasies over the contents of his body seemed quite central to his anxieties at the time of the interview, but it would be difficult to prove that these fantasies existed throughout the months he presented his symptoms. Considering the main points of the consultation, the verbalization of Leon's fantasy seemed to be very important. There had been many times when Mr and Mrs L had tried to get Leon to defecate "properly" with poor results. The fact that they succeeded in their efforts after our meeting must be linked to their recognising that Leon needed strict regularity and persistence on their part and, even more important, finding out how their own childhood experiences had led them to doubt that a child in Leon's situation could be actually helped by the adults around him.

Apparently, it was the recommendation of strict discipline that played a major role in bringing the desired improvement, but this advice had already been given to the parents many times before, without any result. I would argue that the relevant factor in our consultation was the combination of Leon understanding my translation of his anxieties into words and his parents recognising the need to change their attitude of apparent tolerance and kindness to one of clear support and firmness. The promise of the reward probably gave Leon a tangible goal to aim for, and I suppose it also allowed Mr and Mrs L to recognise that they had an active part in the search for success. In other words, instead of being caught up in a vicious circle of despondency and helplessness, they could all engage in a mutually reinforcing circle of encouragement and success.

Eve

Eve was a three-and-a-half-year-old who was referred by the health visitor for night and daytime wetting. An older brother came to the meeting, but sat away in a corner. The mother was the youngest child of a large family and looked pale, worn, and anxious. She had worked for an international organisation, but now stayed at home. The father had a lighter face, with an easy smile; he had a brother and sister, both older than him. He now worked as an artist.

Eve was a pretty blonde girl, who quickly made herself at home. She went straight for the toys on the table. She picked up an elephant and brought it to show me, but refused to answer my questions, only making unintelligible baby noises—to try and provoke me in some way, I thought. She then picked up a bear, held down its ears, and brought it to me, saying "Teddy has no ears". As I began to speak to her parents, Eve held each animal in one hand, turned them upside down and made sure we all saw that she was comparing their underneaths. She then placed each animal next to a doll, both snuggling up into her sides. She stayed watching them for a bit, quite tenderly, making her baby-noises.

Eve had become dry by the age of eighteen months. Not long afterwards, the family went on a summer holiday at the seaside. They described several amusing incidents and, because Eve had resumed bedwetting at that time, they were keen to establish any relevant events that might explain the wetting. An au pair had left them to have a baby at that time and they finally agreed that she had gone in August and the holiday had taken place in September. At the time of the consultation Eve slept in nappies and was reluctant to use the toilet during the day, so that often she got herself wet.

From Eve's play with the animals and the story of the au pair, I believed I knew the nature of the problem, but I needed evidence to justify my interpretation. I asked Eve to draw, but she refused. I asked the father to help but he claimed not to know what to draw. Then he drew a music stand, but suddenly Eve interrupted and asked him to draw a fish (Figure 17):

1. Eve gave him the green felt-tip and when he finished, she got the blue pen and filled it in, very carefully and meticulously (almost centre page).
2. Now Eve gave him the yellow pen and again she filled it in (bottom-left).

Figure 17. Eve's drawing.

3. Eve hesitated and picked up the purple pen. Her father drew "a different" (flat) fish, describing it. Eve said "this is the cross mummy fish"; we all laughed and Eve pointed to number two, saying this was "grumpy" (top-right).
4. Eve asked for a "daddy" fish. Mr E said this would also be different—when Eve saw the long sword, she was surprised. She asked where the mouth was and father explained it did not show because of the sword. Eve was clearly embarrassed and fell silent. She then asked for a "baby" fish (bottom-right).
5. Father did a minute smudge just above number three and Eve objected, demanding something bigger (showing the size with her hands)—she gave him the green pen, he drew it (far left, middle), and she now filled it in.

I was now aware of time running out. I knew what I wanted to say, but I was not sure whether the parents would agree with the "evidence" I could present for my comments. So, I decided to talk directly to Eve: I told her that her mother was right, the nanny's pregnancy was important and it had affected Eve. I called her attention to the fact that she had filled in only the female fish—that is, she knew that something was inside the nanny's body and her examining the underneath of the animals showed that she knew that boys and girls are different, but her comment that "teddy has no ears" probably meant she felt she had something missing. Sounds like too much, but Eve's reaction was to pick up a rabbit puppet and make it kiss me, then she did the same to her mother, on whose lap she now lay down.

Unsurprisingly, both parents were shocked and asked me what the relevance was of what I had said. I explained that she was afraid of the toilet, not knowing what would come out of her. "But she has no problem with the poos", said her mother. I could only answer that perhaps it was "the front" she feared, as she seemed aware of the difference between boys and girls. Luckily, the mother confirmed this, saying it was a subject that Eve had commented on.

The parents wanted to have a definite prescription to help Eve. I said this was probably not necessary, as I believed that it was their knowing of her worries that she needed. But they decided to make a chart, based on which Eve might get a reward. I suggested they should discuss and bargain with Eve about what this reward might be. Eve now told me that she wanted to take the drawing away. As I wanted to keep it, I had to face hard bargaining. She finally accepted borrowing the rabbit puppet as an exchange for the drawing.

When I saw the family again two weeks later, I was told that Eve had not wet herself since our meeting.

Comments

The only relevant factor I could find in the parents' history was the fact that, prior to their own children, they had no experience of child-rearing. It was quite striking that all the details of Eve's play that could be seen as a transparent statement of her unconscious fantasies meant nothing to them. They were caring and devoted parents, but I could not avoid thinking that they would not know how to help a child overcome a "childish" conflict, though it seems that after our initial interview they were prepared—and able—to help Eve overcome her wetting. I should mention that only very rarely would I comment on the unconscious meaning of a parent's contribution, hence my silence on father's choice of a "daddy fish".

Some months later I asked the GP for any news and I was told the family had not consulted them since the interviews with me.

Jennifer

This will not be an account of a consultation along the lines of the other cases presented so far, since Jennifer was not the referred patient. Her story is presented here because of a drawing she made that helped her to recognise and understand her nightmares.

I had been seeing the J family for some time. They had first come to see me because an adolescent daughter had taken a serious overdose. The initial assessment interview with the girl and her mother brought to light an extremely complex family structure and a multiplicity of conflicts. Because Mrs J was concerned about the difficulties affecting several of her children, she insisted that the family should embark on further meetings. This was only partly fulfilled. The adolescent girl who had taken the overdose did improve and managed to resume her school life. Another sibling stumbled from one crisis to another affecting school and social life. An older child seemed to have serious problems but chose to enlist at a provincial university and live away from the family. Marital conflicts had been and continued to be extremely complex and serious.

At a point where a family member turned up unexpectedly from abroad, the intensity and frequency of emotional clashes in the J household reached a new pitch. At this point in time, the family brought Jennifer, aged eight, to their sessions with me. A charming and vivacious little girl, she quickly sensed that there was no room for her to be involved in the discussion, which time and again became quite heated. Jennifer arranged a little corner where she could sit comfortably and use a stool as a working surface, so that she could play with some toys and also draw.

During the second session that Jennifer attended, I noticed that she had made an elaborate and colourful picture. The family discussion had focused on the usual topics, as described above, but the arrival of the family member produced a series of passionate protests and critical comments that must have been difficult for Jennifer to make sense of. During a brief silence, which followed a heated interchange, I asked Jennifer what she had drawn. She beamed and got up to bring the drawing closer to me. "This is a house and this is a little girl—me, really" (Figure 18).

As was to be expected, I asked her questions about the elements in the picture, hoping she would give me the story she had depicted. But what she said was not what I might have expected. "The house is empty, nobody lives there." What kind of house is this, I asked. "A happy house." How do you know? What makes it a happy house?

Figure 18. Jennifer's first drawing.

"The roof—the pattern, the tiles, the colours, all very beautiful, it is a happy house." And the sun? Why is it so low? "It is not low, it's up in the sky." But in that position, I think the girl, you, cannot see it? "Yes, she could, because the house is further back."

Jennifer did not sound impatient or irritated with my questions. She seemed to know precisely what she wanted to answer and she carried on. From my point of view, I was convinced that there was some meaning in the picture that I was not managing to elicit from Jennifer. "Have you ever seen a house like that?", I asked. "No, never." At this point, I asked the question which I turn to in similar situations where the child claims not to know something which I assume she must know, even if not able to recognise it. "Have you perhaps seen such a house in a dream?" "No", said Jennifer. And, quite unexpectedly, Mrs J, who had been following our conversation silently, as had the other family members in the room, spoke to Jennifer: "Tell the doctor about your nightmares". I was taken by surprise, as no reference had been made to this before. Mrs J explained now that Jennifer often wakes up in the night, complaining of terrifying nightmares. After some reluctance, Jennifer told me that in her dreams "people want to take me away from Mummy", but she firmly denied that this would have any connection with the drawing she had made.

I now noticed something unusual in the picture and I invited Jennifer to look at it from a distance. I held the picture up and moved it away from Jennifer. She could not see what I might be pointing to. Then her older sister said "it's a face". Now Mrs J also agreed and remarked on the eyes/windows, but Jennifer still denied seeing anything unusual there. I ended up telling Jennifer that I certainly accepted what she had said, but it still seemed to me that *if* that house ever came up in a dream, it would be very scary. I said that "my story" for that picture would be that the little girl (Jennifer herself) saw this beautiful house and promptly imagined it was a happy house, but suddenly the house turned into this scary, monstrous face—and now the little girl would get really frightened. Jennifer sustained her friendly, somewhat sceptical smile, said nothing and then turned round to get more paper and returned to her corner, clearly wanting to continue drawing.

The family discussion was resumed after a pleasurable hiatus. Siblings continued from where they had stopped and Mrs J again complained about her husband's detachment from the family problems. We carried on, but then I noticed that Jennifer had brought another drawing that she wanted to show me (Figure 19).

Figure 19. Jennifer's second drawing.

She explained, rather shyly, that this was "hugs and kisses"—so, it seemed I had been right after all, and this was a particularly gratifying reward.

According to Mrs J, the nightmares disappeared after this meeting. But the family conflicts continued with repeated crises, which must have aroused time and again Jennifer's anxiety about the future of the family and her own position in it.

Comments

In spite of our psychoanalytic focus on the importance of the interpretation of unconscious feelings, it never fails to surprise me how nightmares and so many other indications of emotional distress can disappear as soon as the person is able to recognise their underlying meaning. One has to recognise that the professional's role is important here. Once the child trusts this person enough to share its conflicts, it becomes the professional's goal to identify the underlying unconscious experience that has been upsetting the child. It is from my experience of cases similar to Jennifer's that I came to see my role as that of a translator—someone who can understand the language of the unconscious and proceeds to provide a translation which the child's conscious mind can understand and recognise (or not!) as valid and effective.

And I was moved and grateful for Jennifer's charming expression of gratitude.

Diana

I was asked to see this delightful twelve-year-old girl because she had developed a very disturbing fear of spiders that had become more intense "in the last few years".

She led a perfectly ordinary, normal life; she was successful at school, had a wide circle of friends, and enjoyed good relationships with her wide family. Both parents had active social and professional lives and, though divorced, had kept a friendly relationship, managing to help Diana to feel happy in their company.

When I interviewed the parents, they told me about their lives, but I could not find any datum that might be significant in helping me to understand Diana's anxieties. They were baffled by the nature and the intensity of her phobic complaints, but they could neither find explanations for it, nor manage to reduce her symptoms. The decision to request the consultation was the result of an episode of panic that surpassed previous occurrences of this: Diana was in her father's car when a "mini-spider" appeared, walking outside the car window. Diana burst out crying and many hours went by before she managed to overcome her panic.

Diana was able to give me a clear account of her life. She had an older sister who suffered from severe and complex pulmonary and heart problems that led to occasional episodes of serious breathing difficulties that often required hospitalisation. These had become more severe in the last three years and, in fact, surgery had been considered, but discussions were still ongoing. Both her parents were in good health and Diana felt very happy and proud of their managing to give her a sense of security and happiness.

Diana told me of the time when she was five years old and she played in the house garden with various plants and animals, including spiders. It was only over the last three or four years that her fear began to affect her. She told me of lying in bed and when seeing her hair against the light coming through the window, she would compulsively try to remove the hair from the light. And as time went on, her fears increased, leading her to avoid places where spiders could appear.

However articulate she was when describing all matters of her daily life, Diana would only shudder and make sounds to indicate fear and panic when referring to spiders. I suggested she should make some drawing. She asked if I wanted anything specific and I said she should feel free to draw anything at all. To my surprise, she drew a spider (Figure 20).

Figure 20. Diana's drawing.

She said that "even the eyes" scare her, but it was the tentacles that represented the greatest threat. Indeed, these were drawn quite elaborately and of a striking size. Bearing in mind the information of her sister's pulmonary crises, I said that, considering the size of the spider's tentacles, it would be quite dangerous to be gripped by them—they could easily suffocate their victim.

Diana now made a drawing of her family members, but this did not show anything remarkable. We agreed on a further appointment, ten days later.

When we next met, I saw a completely different girl. Diana had brought along a couple of plastic spiders and she told me (and her parents confirmed it) that spiders had now become a valued plaything. And when I met Diana a month later, I learnt that she had seen some spiders in their garden and had, in fact, stepped on them with no sign of fear.

Comments

Once aware of the possible chronological coincidence between the appearance of Diana's phobia and the worsening of her sister's breathing condition, this would certainly influence my understanding of her account, and seeing the size of the tentacles she drew, I had no doubt of the connection between her sister's crises and Diana's terror of the damage that a spider might cause. What is so remarkable in this case is the effect of Diana's recognising the menacing tentacles she had depicted on paper. It was I who said the word "suffocate", but it was Diana's unconscious that led her to depict tentacles of that size and structure— and she could now understand how her fears had come into being.

It is this combination of factors that characterises the cases in this collection: the patient's unconscious finds some way of depicting/ conveying its anxiety and, if the professional can recognise and translate this unconscious meaning into words, then relief follows. In Diana's case, the parents' role was not so significant, but in most of the other cases, it is important that they take notice of the child's anxieties and change, accordingly, their manner of dealing with the child.

Alex

The story of this ten-year-old boy will sound as if it is a work of
fiction and I can only affirm that what follows is, truly, what I
found. Alex's parents were divorced and his mother now lived
with a new partner, with whom she had given birth to another child.
Every Friday she took Alex to visit her parents' home and, quite often,
Alex would stay with his grandparents for several days. Alex's father
lived on his own, but the fact that he had had a succession of girlfriends
had occasionally led to conflicts with Alex.

Mrs A and her parents lived in the same neighbourhood and shared
the same GP practice. Alex's problems had led both Mrs A and her parents to request repeated consultations that led to several referrals to
specialists, but no definite organic pathology had ever been identified.
Alex came to see me with his grandparents. A very intelligent and articulate boy, he told me of his various symptoms and it was very striking
how he could remember precisely the day, place, and time when each
abnormality had manifested itself. He told me of sleepwalking and
"quickening"—a type of tremor and shaking that affected limbs and
various other muscles. He was staying at his father's place when this
had happened for the first time: a totally unusual, violent storm had
occurred that night and Alex tried to go to his father's bedroom to ask

for help, but he found the door locked and was afraid of knocking at the door or calling his father.

However, I was told that Alex had "always" had night fears, and this led to his grandparents always leaving their bedroom door open. The Friday night following that first sleepwalking episode, Alex was staying with his grandparents and during the night he again began sleepwalking. This recurred the following nights when he was sleeping at his mother's place. It turned out that his grandfather had suffered from sleepwalking as a child, as well as the "quickening". Not only that, but his grandmother had heart problems and her hands shook quite noticeably. Furthermore, Alex's grandfather knew that his own father had suffered with these complaints and this led him to fear Alex had inherited these abnormalities. Another problem was added: Alex finds it very difficult to fall asleep and he will come out of his bedroom and walk along the corridor, and recently he had been presenting hypnagogic hallucinations—all of which meant that it was not surprising that he would often sleep in the grandparents' bedroom.

I tried very hard to convince Alex and his grandparents of the significance of the negative reports from various specialists. I argued that they were caught up in a vicious circle where each one's behaviour brought forward in the other precisely the confirmation that this behaviour was justified. In other words, the more they "protected" Alex, the more he believed that there was something wrong with him—a sentiment that was bound to affect his self-confidence and his behaviour.

But the family wanted a definite prescription and I urged them to "strike a deal" with Alex, so that he would get a present if he slept seven nights in his own bed. Of course they felt this was a pointless exercise, but when they came to see me two weeks later they told me that Alex had slept in his own bed every night since our first meeting. Alex was very proud of this and his grandparents were pleased and relieved.

We continued our discussion and I was careful not to mention the theoretical possibility that their seeing Alex as in need of protection might also result from their feelings towards Alex's father. This was an easy-going conversation, but I was suddenly told that grandfather wakes Alex up every night to urinate, since he is afraid that Alex might wet his bed. Indeed, Alex had been enuretic years earlier, but grandfather was surprised to hear that Alex spends nights at friends without ever needing to urinate during the night.

Grandmother felt strongly that no further appointments were needed at this point. I pointed out that, ideally, Alex should have some individual psychotherapy sessions to help him cope with the pressures of adolescence, but I was told that they wanted to wait and observe developments.

Comments

I see this boy as proof of how a child's anxieties will find expression in ways that he learns will be understood and responded to by his parents/carers. The presenting complaints are the result of the combination of what is inborn, part of the child's personality, with the input that the child obtains from parents and other close carers. I have at times asked students how they explain the fact of their patient speaking a particular language—of course, he will speak the language he learnt from his parents. And, considering the family dynamics in which Alex grew up, it does not come as a surprise that he "adopted" the problems of both grandparents. I found Alex a very unhappy child who should have the benefit of individual psychotherapy, but sadly this recommendation was not accepted by his family.

I heard from the family's GP some months later that Alex was making good progress and no further consultations had been sought.

Angela*

Angela was first referred to the clinic when she was twenty-five months old. When she attended the health centre for a routine developmental check-up, her mother complained that Angela was presenting increasing difficulties with her eating. The community paediatrician wrote:

> Angela has an eating problem. She survives on numerous snacks during the day and will only take a couple of mouthfuls of food at meal times. Mother says that she has tried various approaches to try and get Angela to eat at meal times. This problem started at around nine months of age and has not improved. Angela has managed, in spite of all this, to sustain good weight gain, remaining just above the fiftieth centile since the age of nine months. My impression is that her mother is a sensible person and she does seem to have approached this problem in a reasonable manner.

---

*Angela's drawings (described in this chapter) were unavailable for reproduction here.

An appointment was sent to Mrs A, but she failed to attend. We spoke to the referring doctor and the family's health visitor and we were told that it might be best not to pursue the referral at that point. One year later, Angela was referred again. The general practitioner told us that Angela, now just over three years old, had an eye test some months earlier; she was shown a picture of a fly and since then had developed a severe "fly phobia" and was terrified of seeing them. She would cry and "pinch herself, refusing to go into any room until she is reassured that there are no flies there".

This time, Angela and Mrs A did attend. Angela curled up into her mother's lap and refused to speak to me. It was Mrs A who recounted Angela's difficulties. The little girl was recovering from German measles and I thought this might be a factor in producing her clinging behaviour and her reluctance to answer any questions. Angela was an attractive child, modestly but neatly dressed, and I could see in her eyes that she was paying attention to every detail of our conversation. For her part, Mrs A was happy to hold Angela lovingly while trying to answer my questions. After a while, I suggested to Angela that she might perhaps make a drawing; she closed her eyes and Mrs A held her just that little bit more closely, giving the impression that there might be here an element of over-protection. Mrs A continued to answer my questions, and after some more minutes, Angela shifted her position and it was clear that she was ready to move away from her mother's lap; indeed she went to the little desk where I kept paper and various kinds of pens.

Both Mrs A and I were near the desk, so that we could follow Angela's drawing. She made something of a circle, where she inserted various features and announced that this was a picture of her father; it looked quite strange, but I made no comment. Angela then said she was going to draw her mother, but now Mrs A became an active participant, asking Angela for each detail of her face. Angela, obligingly, drew in the eyes, nose, etc., and this did look more like a drawing of a face. As Angela developed this drawing, I was asking Mrs A to give me some information about herself and her husband. They had married quite young, but they were now in their late thirties; they had been trying to have children right from the beginning of the marriage, but apparently Mr A had a low sperm count and this was only discovered after many years. Mrs A felt that considerable anxiety had surrounded Angela from birth and this had caused her to be "a spoilt little girl". Mrs A added, laughing in a rather self-deprecatory way, that Angela's childminder was very strict, "which must be good for Angela".

Mrs A told us that she worked as a computer operator, while her husband was an insurance salesman. Though both parents had several siblings, they were aware of the possibility that Angela might remain an only child. Mrs A told me that Angela had long been afraid of flies and spiders, but the incident at the optician's had added a more dramatic level to her anxieties. Angela had "screamed the place down" when she saw a 3-D fly on one of the testing machines and she now refused to enter into any room from the moment she saw a fly there. One of the parents had to kill the fly and Angela would then examine it—but a complication emerged at this point, with Mrs A telling me that she herself was also very frightened of flies and spiders. Angela was following the conversation and I was puzzled by the difference between her alert, shining eyes and the low-key, slow, immature movements of her body and her general demeanour. Her drawing also seemed very immature, in view of this impression of a child who followed the adults' dialogue so attentively.

Angela now moved away from the paper and began to play with the dolls' house. She took off the roof with competent, dextrous movements and began to pick up pieces of furniture that she proceeded to lift and drop into the opening left by the removal of the roof. This was definitely not the noise-making game that some children will carry out—"attention-seeking behaviour", as it tends to be called. Angela picked up some piece of furniture, looked toward her mother and myself, smiled, and dropped it into the house. She clearly wanted to make sure that we were watching her actions. I asked Angela what she was trying to do, what was happening to the various pieces, who was throwing them, and several more questions that remained without answer.

I was puzzled by Angela's play, but Mrs A was even more puzzled by my determination to make something out of it. I just could not figure out what Angela was showing us and I commented on my impression that there was something in Angela's eyes and in her facial expression when throwing the various bits of furniture that made me feel that she was not performing (with her drawings and now in the play with the wooden toys) at the level of her potential. To my surprise, Mrs A smiled and said that she had also noticed that "Angela seems to be acting more babyish than at home". This confirmation made me think that Angela might, quite unconsciously, be recreating some experience for which she lacked the vocabulary to articulate. I asked Angela if she might perhaps be showing us something that happens in her dreams: could it be that frightening things kept falling down in her dreams? Angela smiled, coyly, nodded, and said a quiet "yes". As soon as she said this, she sat down on a little chair and began to play with the furniture inside the house, now trying to organise it in some attractive way, like any other ordinary three-year-old might do. She arranged the furniture and then brought several miniature "people" to sit around a table and enjoy a meal together, making it look like a family meal.

I did not really know how to relate all this to flies and spiders. I decided to call Mrs A's attention to the way in which Angela had repeatedly checked that she was following each detail of her play and, predictably, I was told that probably any child of that age would do the same. I gave what I thought was another example of the same kind of interaction, pointing to Angela's drawing of her mother's face. I wanted to avoid any impression of finding fault with Mrs A's behaviour, so I stressed how Angela cued her into dictating every detail of the face, much in contrast with the way in which she had drawn her father's face. Mrs A, rather reluctantly, agreed with my interpretation. When I thought she had understood my point, I urged her to try and force Angela to follow her own inclination, whatever was involved, instead of giving her any form of guidance as to how to proceed. I added that there was a possibility that Angela might be following the same pattern over the issue of flies and spiders—that is, Angela might be indicating *fear* as a testing out of the mother's reaction to her feelings. If this was the case, then each time Mrs A reacted in a protective way, Angela was bound to believe that there was, indeed, something dangerous that she had to be defended from. Mrs A smiled politely, but I noticed that Angela had followed our conversation and, however much she could have understood of it, she now had a warm, quiet smile on her face.

We had to stop and we arranged a follow-up appointment, but this was postponed by Mrs A who claimed an unexpected family commitment. They came to see me again nearly two months later. The only reference to flies or spiders was Mrs A mentioning that it was no longer a problem. She said that immediately after our first meeting Angela had become "a different child; her normal self". Both parents had noticed that she was "brighter and happier". Angela sat quietly, smiling occasionally, but still refusing to engage with several attempts I made to talk to her. Eventually, Mrs A said that they had a new problem: Angela kept crying in her sleep and all attempts to discover why this was happening had not proved successful.

I suggested that Angela might perhaps like to make a drawing. I gave her some felt-tip pens and paper. She chose a yellow pen and looked up to her mother's face. I promptly signalled to Mrs A to refrain from telling Angela what to draw, and she smiled like a child caught red-handed just about to infringe some rule. Angela drew an irregular oval shape and moved back from the desk. She looked round, making sure that we were watching her. She leant forward toward the paper, still holding the pen and this time she moved briskly away: the body movement pointed to fear or some similar emotion, even though her face showed a mischievous smile. She repeated these movements again and, by the third time, her body was contorted, as if in terror. I asked her what she had drawn and this time she told me it was "a moo-cow". Before saying anything to Angela, I checked with Mrs A whether she had observed how Angela had made her drawing, particularly the body movements she had made. Very calmly, Mrs A confirmed she had seen all this and added that she could explain what was going on.

Only a few days earlier, the family had gone on a drive to the country and they had at one point suddenly come against a herd of cows being moved along a road, and this had terrified Angela. As far as I could tell, Mrs A had not made any connection between Angela's behaviour (perhaps we can say her "body language") and the story she had told me. Apparently, from her point of view, she wanted me to know why a "moo-cow" had been drawn. I said that Angela had treated *the drawing* as if it was a real cow. Mrs A did not hide her disbelief and, anyway, even if I was right, how could this interpretation be relevant? I explained that with the drawing and her reaction, Angela might be showing us what was happening in her dreams. Angela nodded vigorously and said an emphatic "yes". Very significantly, Mrs A now smiled in a way which, very eloquently, indicated that if Angela had confirmed my interpretation, then this sufficed for her to recognise and accept that this was correct. Angela must have read her mother's face in the same way as I did, because she moved away from the desk and went over to snuggle into her mother's lap.

Mrs A commented that "it was quite astonishing" that a little three-year-old could find a way of conveying her experiences to me, even when lacking the words to express them. They left quite happily and we learnt some weeks later from the health visitor that Angela had not had any further problems and that Mrs A kept telling people of the "magical" interchange between Angela and myself.

We heard from Angela and Mrs A again, two years later. Angela was having nightmares and Mrs A's anxiety was heightened by the fact that a crisis situation had developed at school. Somehow, Angela's teachers thought she was colour-blind and also presented a speech defect; apparently, Mrs A had tried to argue with them that neither assertion appeared justified, but the teachers insisted on medical checks being carried out. Ophthalmic tests proved negative, but Angela still had to have the speech assessment. Probably because of the success of our earlier meetings, Mrs A requested a new appointment with me.

Angela seemed to recognise me, but she was just as monosyllabic as when we first met. Mrs A, for her part, remained enmeshed with Angela, quite incapable of keeping herself back whenever she gave the slightest indication of needing or wanting her mother's help. Angela had grown and seemed a confident child, but all my questions were answered with "I don't know ...", which might vary in tone, but not in words. Each time, she would look towards her mother, who promptly plunged into some kind of explanation. It was clear that Mrs A's anxiety was growing exponentially. I would guess that it was this brand of helplessness on Angela's part that had raised the teachers' concern, but it was also possible that the teachers saw her mother's level of anxiety as a further factor in Angela's difficulties.

As two years earlier, I resorted to pens and paper. Luckily, Angela accepted my suggestion. She drew a boat, lying tilted on its side. I tried many different questions to elicit what exactly that boat was meant to represent—"I don't know" was always the answer. Eventually, she said it was "a blue and red boat". I commented that she had used other, different colours and she confirmed this but could not (or would not) clarify why she had only chosen red and blue to name the boat. Very slowly and hesitantly, Angela noticed that she had forgotten to draw any water around the boat, but did not add it. Then she said it was on some path, though to me it looked as if the boat was floating on air, with no features around it to give any clue to its location. She said: "When the wind blows it sails faster ... when the wind is slow, it goes slow ... when it rains, the people jump out of the boat on to the path". I then asked more questions: is anything happening? Or had anything already happened? The boat was so tilted—why? Was it lost? Is it in the sea? Then, rather unexpectedly, Angela said the boat had fallen over because the wind had blown too fast—and added, "end of story". I was truly stuck. "You said people jumped on the path—what will they do?" "They work". So, what next? I asked "what kind of story is this: is it funny or sad?", and she replied without hesitation: "It's sad, because of the boat …".

I asked whether she had seen this story in a book or on television? Had she made it up herself? Or could it be a dream? Having answered my questions in the negative, she now confirmed my last one without delay: "It's a dream I had". Because Angela had said it was the boat's situation that made for sadness, I ventured an interpretation, asking her whether she was perhaps afraid of being left alone, like the boat. Angela smiled, coyly, but her mother promptly jumped, telling me that only a few days ago Angela had told her of a dream: they had seen some balloons in the street when returning home from school, and in her dream Angela was holding on to a balloon by its string, while the balloon appeared to take her away into the air. I put the two explanations together and suggested that Angela might be afraid of not being held, or being allowed to get out of reach, of losing contact. Poor Mrs A was suddenly beside herself—could this fear be related to her now working full-time? Angela goes to a childminder after school, "but I'm never late!", and soon "Do you think I should stop working? Will she be less afraid?"

I explained that it was unlikely that we were dealing with actual events that called for immediate remediation and suggested that Angela knew quite well that her mother would not neglect her, but it could have happened that one day Mrs A was a bit late and Angela formed the impression that she might not come anymore. Angela, who had not missed a single word of this conversation, nodded vigorously. Mrs A now remembered that the childminder's son had "only the other day" joked with Angela that her mother would not come for her. Curiously, exactly as two years earlier, Angela now relaxed quite visibly and moved over to the other side of the table to play with the various toys.

I discussed with Mrs A what to do next. I could not think that any tests would reveal any particular abnormality, but I encouraged her to comply with the teachers' requests. I explored the possibility of offering Angela some psychotherapy, but Mrs A was quite determined not to have any more interventions than those she decided were absolutely indispensable. She refused a follow-up appointment with the powerful argument that she had come back for further help when she thought this necessary—she reassured me she would do so again, if the need arose.

Comments

I fear that Angela would have to struggle very hard to achieve some independence from her mother. Mrs A had a very low level of tolerance for anxiety, particularly when Angela was involved, and this made it virtually impossible for her to appreciate Angela's behaviour as pertaining to a separate person. Mrs A was bound to continue with the ordinary commitments characteristic of her age and her social class, whether for economic reasons or because of some unconscious need to establish some distance from her daughter. Sadly, this made her feel extremely guilty when Angela showed signs of distress and, as our interviews showed, her emotional turmoil only led to further anxiety in Angela. Fortunately, our meetings succeeded in breaking this vicious circle: Angela could understand what her dreams meant and finding her fears translated into words seemed to relieve her symptoms, whilst Mrs A seemed to find my words reassuring enough for her to continue what was, undoubtedly, her good-enough care of Angela. However, I would anticipate further crises as Angela made her progress through late childhood and adolescence.

Henry

The family's GP asked me to see this ten-year-old boy because, since watching a horror film ("The Candyman") some two or three years earlier when visiting some relations, he had developed intense feelings of anxiety. This interfered with his sleeping patterns and he found it very difficult to be on his own during the night. Henry's family consulted a psychiatrist who recommended long-term therapy with a psychotherapist, but the GP suggested they should see me for a second opinion.

Henry had two brothers, one older and one younger. Mr H was in his late forties, working in the world of finance, and Mrs H, of the same age, had worked as a nurse, but then devoted herself to bringing up her children. Henry came with his mother to see me. He was a good-looking boy of average height, with bright, inquisitive eyes, who made himself at home without much difficulty. He knew why he had been brought to see me and he clearly saw me as a professional who might be able to help him. He was well aware of what he wished to convey to me and his domain of ideas and words was very striking. Some of his sentences were so perceptive and concise that I have never forgotten them, and yet, even if addressed to me, much of what he said seemed to reflect flowing, tormenting formulations of his experiences and thoughts.

Henry told me of seeing "flashes", images of ghosts, and other indefinable figures that, as soon as he became aware of them, produced intense anxiety. When they occurred at school, he had learnt to "get my mind on to something else", but when they appeared while he was at home, he did not manage to "concentrate" and could not remain in his own bed. He would go out in search of his mother, who slept on the floor below. If she was not in her bed, he would go to his siblings' bedroom. Having been told that his mother sometimes worked and studied in a room on the ground floor of their house, I asked Henry why did he not go down to that floor. "Oh, because if she was not there, I would have to go back up all the stairs", which he clearly thought was a valid justification. However, if he found his mother on her bed, he laid down by her side, feeling comforted and safe.

I asked if other significant events had occurred at the time when Henry had seen the film. He replied that his grandfather had died around that time. His mother was unable to clarify the chronology of these events, but she told me that his death had been quite unexpected—he had suffered a heart attack when driving his car. I asked if there had been any more deaths. Much to Mrs H's surprise, Henry told me that many years earlier, when abroad on holiday, they had come home one day to find the housekeeper dead in the swimming pool. He did not remember witnessing the event, but he had not forgotten it.

Considering these stories where people were found to have died with no warning or possibility of obtaining help, I came to the suspicion that Henry was frightened of death. I said "it seems you are afraid of death", and I heard the remarkable, memorable phrase: "I'm not afraid of death—I am afraid of dying". I was so impressed by this statement that I did not immediately appreciate how central this was as an explanation of Henry's repeated crises of anxiety.

Henry made a drawing of the "Candyman" (Figure 21) where he wrote "very still face". Both Mrs H and I asked about the facial features. "I can see it, but I wouldn't be able to draw it." We were surprised by this and muttered words to indicate our failure to understand this specific difficulty. Henry, quite forcefully, asked us: "Do you remember your great-grandmother? Do you remember your grandfather? You would find it very difficult to draw the face of anyone whom you've seen briefly—you try to remember, but all the details get mixed up together".

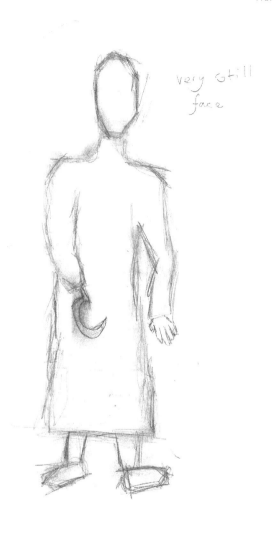

very still
face

11.10.99

Figure 21. Henry's drawing.

I thought this was a statement of how he could not distinguish the facial features of housekeeper, his grandfather, and Candyman—nor of whoever else was to die next. And I thought this was the reason for not wanting to lose sight of his mother. As I was putting these ideas into words, Mrs H told me that the previous weekend she had given Henry a present and, somehow, he had slept through the following night. I said this was an important point to take into account and suggested she should establish a system of rewards for nights when Henry stayed in his bed, but definitely not to allow him to sleep on her bed. As I do in similar cases, I explained the paradoxical effect of what many parents see as a sign of love and protection: letting the child sleep on their bed is felt as a confirmation that the child does face a real danger he must be protected from.

Mrs H phoned me three days later. After seeing me, she had to take Henry to his bed for two nights, but the previous night he had stayed in his bed and, at breakfast time, all the family congratulated him and father gave him some money as a reward. Mrs H added her admiration for the drawing her son had made: "he is good at art, but it was quite incredible what he drew for you".

Henry asked to see me again and we met one month later (after my being away on holiday). He confirmed that he had made some progress, but he wanted to quantify this. He lifted and moved sideways his left hand and said: "I was bad, like here ... now I'm better [as he lifted his right hand] but I would like to improve further [and moved his right hand outwards]". Mrs H told me that, since seeing me, Henry had gone to his bed and fallen asleep with no trouble, but that he had slept the whole night on his own bed only a few nights, while going to his siblings' room most nights. But it seemed that the notion of size was important for Henry. He now told us that he has only short dreams and asked Mrs H if she also had such short dreams. She was puzzled, but Henry went on to explain that short dreams (and he was using his hands to emphasise their size/length) do not bother him. He wakes up and knows all is well. No, the content of the dreams is not relevant, only the length.

Henry picked up a sheet of paper and drew lines of different lengths, representing specific times during the night, trying to show me what he had in mind regarding "short" and not long dreams. I could not really understand the subtlety of his words and drawings. At my request, he drew his family and the only striking point was that his legs did not end at the bottom of the page and he used another sheet (after asking me for permission to do this) to draw his ankles and feet. We spoke about how tall his siblings were and how tall he imagined he would become. I decided to ask him if he had had any thoughts about our earlier meeting, particularly around the issue of death. "Not all the time", he answered. I mentioned his phrase "not afraid of death, only of dying" and, surprisingly, he became rather excited, as if he had to justify this sentiment. He asked me and his mother "if you had to die from a bullet on the head or having each finger pulled out, then each toe pulled out, and then, bit by bit, each bit of your body—which would you choose?" Mrs H addressed me: "He asks this question quite often, you know?" I thought I had come to a conclusion about all these accounts and asked Henry: "Do you know that you said it is not the content of the dream that wakes you up? I suspect that you wake up and then you don't know whether you are really alive or not. And this is why you go searching to see if the others are still alive and make sure that you, yourself, are also alive." Surprisingly, he nodded—"I think this is it"—and went on to repeat each one of my words.

Mrs H requested another appointment one month later. She insisted Henry was much better, but she wanted me to see him again. I was surprised to find that Henry was ill at ease and very fidgety—definitely different from the boy I had seen earlier—and I wondered what had changed. Mrs H stressed her concern that so many nights he will go to sleep on the bed of one of his siblings. He could not explain to me what was the cause for this move: it was nothing to do with bad dreams, he said, and he seemed to have forgotten my interpretation about ensuring whether everyone was still alive.

Henry told me that he had woken up that morning and gone downstairs, finding his father watching television. Mrs H corrected him—she was sure this had happened in the middle of the night and it must have been dark. After some discussion, the subject became Henry's fear of the dark and it now emerged that he watches his bedroom window with fear, scared that someone might come through it—"How can you know when someone wants to murder you?", he asked. Mrs H was clearly annoyed, but went on to mention a friend of his saying that Henry is obsessed with death, killing, war games, etc. I decided to ask about what kind of film does Mr H watch. Henry told us of a recent one where a psychiatrist killed the husband of a patient of his, to please her. But he denied any connection between this and his anxieties.

I voiced my impression that the earlier juxtaposition of death and fear of sleeping seemed to be easing off. I raised again the possibility of a rewards scheme and mentioned the possible advantage of Henry reading something when going to sleep. Henry's response surprised me: he addressed his mother and asked whether perhaps she might make it more difficult for him to leave his room by closing the door when he goes to sleep. Mrs H responded by asking: "Do you want me to close it when you go to bed, or later on?" I could not understand this, and she explained that she will check each child's bed two or three times every night. She was shocked by my comment that this routine might be interpreted (at least by Henry) as proof that something does need checking. She said that she would try and stop doing this.

Mrs H phoned me a week later and said that Henry seemed to be less anxious and he was staying in his own bed through most nights. She felt that no further appointments were needed. It was about one year later that I wrote to Mrs H, asking how Henry was getting on. "He is a happy boy. He never looked back. No problems there!"

Comments

I do believe that the turning point in Henry's night-time problems was his gaining insight on how his behaviour stemmed from his fear of dying. What surprised me in this case was the late discovery of how his mother dealt with her anxiety about her children's sleeping. I do believe that her changing this habit was an important contributor to Henry's managing to sleep through the nights. I did not think it would be proper to contact the family after my last letter and the resultant positive feedback, but I have wondered how Henry developed through his adolescence. The intensity of his fears and the apparent underlying difficulty in distinguishing between fact and fantasy did leave me wondering whether this was an inborn characteristic of his psychological make-up that might come to the surface again in later years.

Peter

This is a case that shows the complexity of the role a parent can play in the development of a child. It is important to remember that the professional only comes to know what he is told. Being human, we cannot avoid building our own interpretation of what we hear and see, but only the people involved have full knowledge of the events they report. And a further, unavoidable, and difficult complication comes to be the simple fact that each one of the family members consulting us may have his own recollection of any specific event—and these versions may be different from each other.

It was the paediatrician who asked me to see Peter, then nearly four-and-a-half years old. His referral letter showed very clearly that he had taken a detailed history of the child's development. Peter had two older brothers: one was breast-fed for ten months and the next one for twelve months; both were developing well, presenting no problems. Peter, however, was breast-fed for twenty-one months, this prolongation being "convenient, to get him off to sleep" (mother's words). The paediatrician wrote that: "it is perhaps no accident that as we were talking, Peter began to be increasingly attention-seeking and then buried his head repeatedly in Mrs P's breast". Mrs P had followed her GP's advice and stopped putting Peter in nappies, but Peter now tried to stop himself from going to the toilet in the morning by crossing his legs and, when forced to empty his bowels, he would do it in his pants. However, it was noteworthy that he never messed himself at school or anywhere outside home. Peter used to wet his bed, but had now stopped this.

The paediatrician thought that the fact of Peter being the last child had played a major role in Mrs P's attachment to him. He urged Mrs P to implement a fixed routine of toilet use and prescribed medication that might help Peter to excrete his stools. But he also recommended a referral to me and Mrs P agreed to have this child psychiatric assessment.

Peter was a healthy looking, attractive boy, who quickly made himself at home, quite happy to tell me stories and answer my questions. Mrs P did not disguise her reaction to her son's stories, but she never corrected him. Peter told me about his siblings and his parents, and after a while he picked up a pen and made a drawing (Figure 22).

Figure 22. Peter's drawing.

To my mind, this revealed very clearly the nature of his anxiety and it was simply fascinating to see how he came to recognise that his drawing showed how scared he was of falling into and being sucked into the toilet. He went on to tell me that these fears had started one day when one of his brothers was reading stories to him while he sat on the toilet.

Mrs P was a teacher and she could recognise the meaning and significance of her son's drawings—and yet, I thought, she did not quite believe that all this was relevant to understand the boy's problems. We discussed some of these ideas and Mrs P came to mention that not a single person in her family had ever had such irrational thoughts. Nevertheless, much to my amazement, Mrs P went on to ask whether I would include superstitions in the same category of irrationality—she then proceeded to tell me of her fear of going under stairs. To our surprise, Peter's reaction showed he could see the relevance of his mother's comment, and before long we had reached a deal: mother and son agreed that both of them would try and challenge the object of their fears.

Peter and his mother came to see me a week later. Peter's fears? Little if any change. But what about Mrs P? It turned out that she had not really managed to put to the test her fears of going under stairs; this was a very difficult meeting, since I did not feel it would be correct to "take Mrs P to task". But further discussion led to the possibility that change might still occur. When I saw them again, ten days later, I was told that Peter had succeeded in using the toilet effectively a few times, though this did not happen every day. Looking at the wider picture, I was rather convinced that the Ps were not a family where routine, discipline, and timetables were so strictly observed—there was love and togetherness, undoubtedly, but they followed the pattern of families who advocate "individual rights", allowing each child to establish his or her own rhythm. It happened, however, that Mrs P mentioned that Peter had developed an ear infection, for which he had been prescribed an antibiotic, the taste of which he hated.

Hearing of this reaction of Peter's, I decided to try a different strategy. As I was seeing them in a general hospital, I excused myself and went to the pharmacy, where I consulted the pharmacist in charge. Could he give me some substance that would produce a strong taste, but that would have no secondary effects? Gentian violet, he said, and gave me a spray with a highly diluted solution of this. I went back to my room and told Peter and his mother that I had managed to obtain a spray that he would use each time he failed to use the toilet properly. Obviously, feeling the strong taste of the spray, he would probably take this as a punishment, so I stressed that this was a memory-strengthening drug that would help him to remember how he was expected to use the toilet. We agreed another appointment for two weeks later.

But Mrs P telephoned the hospital and spoke to my secretary, cancelling the appointment. She said that Peter was now using the toilet every morning, without difficulty and without any fuss. She made it quite clear that she was very surprised by this result, but relieved and somewhat proud as well.

Comments

Once it became clear that parental input could not be relied upon, the challenge was finding some way of enabling Peter to overcome his problem. Peter had gained insight into his problems in a most unusual way, but being aware of what made him avoid using the toilet had not been sufficient for him to overcome his fear. Nevertheless, he was not giving up his fight and I would not be able to explain convincingly why so many oscillations kept occurring. It is conceivable that Peter had, consciously or unconsciously, recognised that the fight was now no longer with his mother, but rather within himself over his own ambivalence regarding success or danger. The unpleasant spray may have acted as a threat to his fear-holding self or, in line with my explicit formulation, a reinforcement for the normality-seeking self.

A successful case, but I regret not having a long-term follow-up on Peter's development. A final question: could we ever establish whether Mrs P's phobic anxieties ("superstitions") played any influence on Peter's developing his fears?

Gloria

This is a brief story that shows very clearly how sensitive a child is to her parents' anxieties. I was asked to see Gloria when she was five years old. She had gone to a summer camp organised by her school and the very next day, claiming that a colleague had been "horrible" to her, she panicked and demanded that the teachers called her parents to take her home. The parents did go and brought her back, and she did feel safer and more protected when in their company.

But when term resumed, Gloria was most resistant to leave home. She would cry and claim all sorts of physical pains. She had recently been seen by an ENT specialist because of "glue ears", and when the family contacted him about Gloria's complaints, and asked him for advice, he suggested a consultation with a professional and gave them my name. Both parents brought Gloria to see me. She was a pretty, self-contained girl, rather shy and very happy to let her parents tell me their version of events and answer my questions. Whatever I asked her, Gloria would shrug her shoulders and give me a brief, not very informative answer. But she never corrected any of her parents' words.

Mr G was in his late thirties, and was a successful lawyer. His family had come from a Far Eastern country and lived away from London. He had a sister and healthy parents. A grandmother had died, and his eyes filled with tears as he told me of reassuring her that her body was here, ill, but God wanted to have her soul next to Him in heaven.

Mrs G was in her mid-thirties. She was a successful administrative officer. The youngest of six children, she told me that all were married and had children, except for one, who was having trouble conceiving. But Mr G commented that her husband did not want children and she was "accepting" this because of her total opposition to a divorce. Our discussion then focused entirely on children. The Gs had married ten years earlier and, once they decided to have a child, Mrs G had become pregnant without difficulty. But when Gloria was born, she was considered dangerously underweight and immediate investigations were started. Mrs G mentioned specifically the placenta being sent to a specialised hospital to check for abnormalities. Whenever recounting something related to present-day events, each time she referred to her daughter, Mrs G would add "she is an only child". I was totally convinced that both husband and wife were unable to believe that they would have a second child.

An unexpected detail was my being told that Mrs G had given Gloria a present the previous day: a dog with four puppies inside it. Yes, Gloria liked it, but kept referring to it as a "he". Mr G told me of his discussions with Gloria's headmistress: he had told her that Gloria refused to get dressed or have breakfast, definitely not to go to school—and the headmistress replied that he should just bring her to school as she was, since they would be able to dress her up for the day. He decided to follow her advice: he had taken Gloria to school the day before they were seeing me. I congratulated him and urged him to continue with his new approach.

We arranged to meet again ten days later, but Mr G phoned and said that they had no further troubles—Gloria was now going to school without any difficulty. I heard from my ENT colleague a few months later that Gloria was attending school normally.

Comments

I believe that it is quite obvious that Gloria was aware of her mother's anxieties, and of the role that she herself played in her mother's life. The parents' attempts to comfort and protect Gloria were probably being experienced by her as a confirmation of the extent to which her presence was valued and needed. It was Mr G's firmness in getting Gloria to school that helped her to feel "allowed" to be away from home.

Unfortunately, I have no information as to whether the Gs managed to have another child, nor about Gloria's long-term development.

Carol*

The general practitioner referred Carol, aged four, for a psychiatric assessment, because:

> … in the last three weeks she wakes up in the night, screaming and then goes into a trance-like state; her teachers say she is disruptive and naughty at school. Her mother has been advised by the school to seek professional help. Carol has had sodium cromoglycate and more recently terbutaline sulphate for chronic coughs and coughing on exercise, that I thought was asthma. We think she had chickenpox one month ago.

The phrasing of the letter clearly indicated that the doctor was agreeing to the referral, whilst reserving his views about the need for such a consultation: Carol's school had recommended help, and Mrs C was prepared to accept this, so the doctor complied. An appointment was sent for Carol and her parents to come to the clinic.

---

*Previously published in *Untying the Knot* (Brafman, 2001) under the name "Mary". This is now a shorter, slightly modified version.

In fact, only Carol and her mother attended for the appointment. After the usual steps of greeting them and trying to make them feel comfortable, Carol moved towards the table with toys and Mrs C told me that, from her point of view, her daughter had two different problems: her disturbed sleep and her "impossible behaviour" at home and at school.

Mrs C was in her late thirties, though she looked much younger. She had worked as a teacher until Carol's birth and she now had a second child, aged one. A sister lived nearby, and she also had a brother who lived abroad. Mr C was a computer designer, also in his late thirties; he was described as a quiet man who avoided confrontations at all costs. Mrs C saw this as a problem when he tried to pacify Carol, rather than disciplining her firmly, as Mrs C would like him to do. The couple had met when both of them were working abroad and they had lived in other countries for several years, before returning home to England. When Mrs C became pregnant with her second child, the couple decided to move to another house and this had taken place quite recently.

Mrs C told me that Carol had always been difficult: "[she] will never do as she is told", "she is disobedient, defiant, always running around". When Carol went to a local nursery, Mrs C felt that "the teachers didn't like her", to judge from comments they had made. Mrs C had visited the nursery and thought that the children were left to their own devices, never properly helped to concentrate on constructive activities. She moved Carol to another nursery, but, again, she was told that Carol was never still, did not obey the teachers, etc. Regarding life at home, she said that Carol "turns every minor daily chore into a big issue", and Mrs C cited Carol refusing to put her shoes on as an example. If Mr C is home and gets involved, Mrs C complained that he "just takes her off to do something different", which Mrs C considered a sign of disrespect for her authority, besides allowing Carol to ignore her responsibilities as a growing child. I was left in no doubt that Mrs C felt intensely challenged and disrespected by Carol, and by her husband.

Though I did not make it explicit, I thought that the couple's age and the years they had spent without having to care for children might have influenced their feelings when facing the subsequent task of bringing them up. Considering the moves the family had made before and after Carol's birth, and also the recent arrival of a younger sibling, I asked whether Mrs C thought these events might have influenced the couple's life, as well as Carol's development. Mrs C did not think this was relevant. She was trying hard to hide her impatience with the questions I asked about herself and her husband. There was no ignoring the fact that Mrs C thought that there was "something wrong" with Carol, and this was what she wanted me to take as my starting point, if not the only focus of my attention.

Carol had been playing with various toys on a table in a quiet and competent manner and I called Mrs C's attention to this, asking her if this was in any way significant. She became quite upset and asked me if I was telling her that she was wasting my time. I explained that what had occurred to me was the possibility that, when interested in something, Carol was able to concentrate and play in a constructive way—in other words, perhaps the nursery was not giving her adequate stimulation. Mrs C dismissed this out of hand, reminding me of what happened all the time at home. I thought that Mrs C's anxiety about Carol seemed out of proportion to the examples she was giving me, but I found no way of reassuring her or of obtaining any clues to what might be causing such intense worry in her. I was struck by the fact that Carol responding so well to her father's approach was taken as a provocation rather than a reassurance, but again I found no room to explore this further.

Mrs C told me about the night-time crises: Carol starts to scream and one or both parents try to wake her up, but even when she stops screaming, Carol will go into a kind of trance which the parents cannot affect, until eventually she returns to sleep. Mrs C had no idea how best to deal with these episodes. While I might be interested in what caused these episodes, Mrs C wanted to know how to eliminate them. I am sure she was concerned by Carol's distress, but she made it sound as if it was the disturbance of the family's sleep that she objected to.

During this conversation, Carol had been playing with the dolls' house. She had arranged some pieces of furniture to make up a kitchen and breakfast room. A daddy and a mummy were preparing breakfast for the baby and a little girl, who were playing together. She managed to stand the wire dolls neatly against the kitchen counter and she was muttering words to indicate a friendly conversation between the parents, occasionally moving over to the children and then making them play in a similar, friendly fashion. I was struck by the dexterity with which she moved the toys and the quiet tone of the events unfolding in the game. After a while, Carol decided to play with something else and she explored the materials on the table. I offered her some jigsaw puzzles, but she dismissed them. She did not seem to like the other toys, and I asked her if she would perhaps like to draw—her face lit up with a wonderful smile. I gave her some sheets of paper and a pack of felt-tip pens and she promptly chose one. She held it firmly and proceeded to draw a circle (Figure 23) and various lines inside and outside of it. (N.B.—most of the dots on this picture were actually made towards the end of the interview).

I could recognise the shapes of a mouth, eyes, a nose, and legs, but I decided to check on those coming out of the side of the face. "Arms!" Carol said, almost angrily, as if I had doubted whether she knew what she had drawn. I asked if the picture showed someone in particular and she said "Mummy". What about the spots on the face? "To make her look nice." She now pushed the paper aside and made another drawing (Figure 24): a spider.

This one took less time to make and she promptly moved on to the next sheet (Figure 25), drawing a frog with a tail and a "turtle fish". Carol could not or did not want to give any explanations about her chosen subjects, though her choice of colours and the determination

Figure 23. Carol's first drawing.

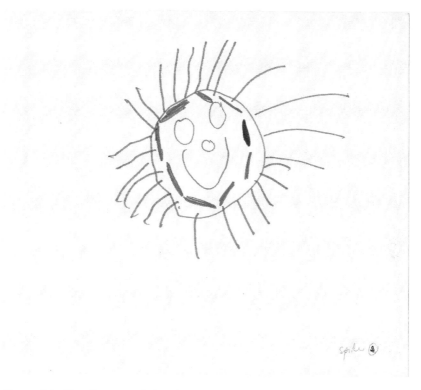

Figure 24. Carol's second drawing.

with which she drew her shapes would point to her having a firm idea
about what was on her mind. Figure 26 depicts money and the numbers
are buttons.

The next drawing (Figure 27) was quite elaborate. She first made the
yellow circles with tail-like lines coming out of them, then the long row
of red circles running in parallel to the yellow circles. She put some
red and blue lines inside the yellow shapes and then more yellow circles with lines at the top of the page, followed by red ones underneath.
Finally, she added the scribbles on the top-left of the picture, drawn
with quite a different movement of the hand. I asked her to explain
what she had drawn and Carol told me about the various elements, but
she slowly moved away from the table and sat down on a nearby settee,
still explaining the drawing, but now also showing me her foot at the
same time. The yellow circles are "rocks"; these are stones where crabs
can hide underneath, but then they come out and "pinch your foot",

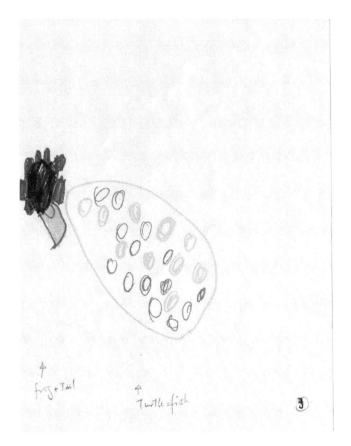

Figure 25. Carol's third drawing.

which is very painful. After a pause, I asked about the scribbles on the top-left of the page and Carol explained this was her name.

Carol went back to the table and drew (Figure 28) with relish, perhaps even excitement. She made a crab with many crabs/circles inside. She explained that the little crabs grow bigger and bigger. She then drew the circles outside the original one. Finally, she made some shapes which she called "letters". As she finished these, she put the pen down and sat back on the chair, making it quite clear that she had no wish to make any further drawings.

Mrs C had followed this sequence with interest, though her face showed her bafflement, perhaps wondering what would come out of all this. I asked her what she had made of the drawings and she made

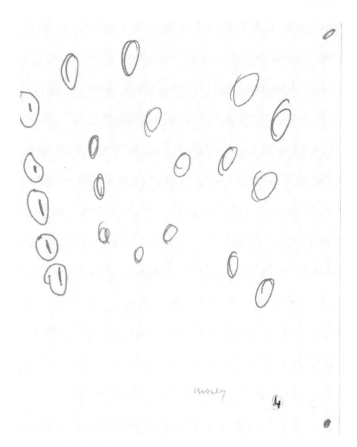

Figure 26. Carol's fourth drawing.

a dismissive face, adding "nothing, really". I explained to Mrs C that I wanted to ask Carol some questions, but that I was keen not to put words in her mouth. I went through each drawing with Carol, to make sure I had understood her descriptions. I then put forward my translation of the pictures: I commented on the fact that the shapes she had used for money, buttons and crabs were all similar circles and Carol nodded her head, as if this should have been obvious. I asked her whether there was any connection between these circles and the dots she had put on the first picture. She nodded vigorously, saying an emphatic "yes" and, picking up the green pen, proceeded to put more and more dots on "mother's" face. Mrs C now looked bewildered, almost irritated, at my encouraging Carol to continue her drawing nonsense. I tried to engage

Figure 27. Carol's fifth drawing.

Figure 28. Carol's sixth drawing.

Mrs C's interest in the content of the pictures, but she definitely failed to see any significance in them.

I now had a difficult problem. However much Mrs C could recognise that Carol was engaged in some meaningful communication with me, I felt quite convinced that she was not pleased with my apparently ignoring the problems that she considered important. By now, I was sure that Mrs C was bound to dismiss any advice I might come to give her regarding Carol's problems. I thought that she had sensed, quite correctly, that I saw Carol's behavioural problems as secondary to her emotional conflicts and that it was these emotional elements that had monopolised my attention. Mrs C wanted a clear medical diagnosis of Carol's condition and a prescription that would not involve anyone other than Carol herself. But, however aware I was of these feelings of Mrs C, I felt unable to forget the fact that Carol had done her best to convey her feelings to me and I did not want to let her down. I was quite worried that Mrs C might object to what I wanted to say, but I decided to take the risk, in the hope that this might help Carol to deal with her anxieties.

I said to Carol that I thought her drawings showed what happened in her dreams: at the beginning, her mother had "a nice face", but then spots appeared on it that gradually turned into dangerous, attacking, hurtful crabs. I added that Carol might be afraid that it was she herself who was hurting and upsetting her mother. It was at this point of my explanation that Carol went back to her first drawing (Figure 23) and inserted a multitude of further dots on the "mother's face". If we wanted to pick out an element of hostility in Carol's feelings towards her mother, these "further injuries" would represent the best evidence—if she was afraid of hurting her mother, here would be the corresponding unconscious wish to inflict such hurt. If I had been seeing Carol alone, I might have voiced this interpretation, but I would not make this explicit when her mother was sitting next to us. I mentioned the suspected "chickenpox" that Carol had suffered some weeks earlier as the source of the "dots on the face" as signs of some damage.

Mrs C now voiced her disbelief with barely contained anger. What I had said was absurd and too far-fetched to be true. I suggested she might ask Carol what she thought and, as Mrs C did this, Carol nodded vigorously, saying that yes, this was how her dreams were. Mrs C appeared to believe Carol's words and I was relieved at this demonstration of trust and acceptance. I tried to explain to Mrs C that children tend to create their own interpretations of their daily experiences, but some of these constructions are relegated to the child's unconscious, so that when they turn up in dreams children can be very frightened, as if their worst fears were turning into reality. There was a possibility that Carol's facial lesions from the recent possible chickenpox had led her to consider them as a sign of badness or danger. Mrs C tried hard to show a polite attitude to these explanations, which were clearly not very convincing to her, but Carol was now quite relaxed and peaceful, again playing with the dolls' house, as if giving us time to round off the interview.

I offered Mrs C the opportunity to ask me any questions, as she seemed to want something quite different from our meeting, but she could not find anything to say. I thought she might want to see me without Carol being present and I offered to see her again on her own or with her husband. Besides trying to offer Mrs C an opportunity to discuss how best to approach the issue of disciplining Carol, I also was interested to discover the source for Mrs C's conviction that Carol harboured some serious pathology. In the event, Mrs C just said she "would think about it and speak to her husband" and let me know of their decision.

One week later, Mrs C telephoned the clinic and said that, since the day of the consultation, Carol had not had any further nightmares and she was now sleeping through the night. Regarding further appointments, she said these were not necessary for the time being. I telephoned the GP some weeks later and he told me that Mrs C had been to see him for some problem with the baby and she had then told him that Carol was sleeping normally. I did not obtain any follow-up regarding Carol's behaviour at school.

Comments

I see Carol's case as evidence for my belief that the help a child gets is entirely dependent on the particular professional who sees her. Though Carol's nightmares caused her parents considerable distress, her mother was mostly worried about her behaviour and this had been the element that determined the school's advice for help to be sought. Had Mrs C been referred to a psychologist who focused on behaviour modification, this would have been the treatment Carol would have received. A paediatrician might have prescribed some tranquilising medication, much as another psychologist could have opted for some counselling for Mrs C, and an educational psychologist might have decided to work with Carol's teachers during visits to the school. Mrs C's account of her clashes with her husband were sufficient indication for some marital counselling. At the end of the day, Mrs C wanted something done *with* and *for* Carol. It is quite conceivable that, whatever benefit followed from my intervention, Mrs C still sought further consultations with other professionals regarding Carol's problems.

I have no doubt that had Carol been referred to a psychoanalytic colleague, the interview was bound to have followed quite a different course, but the moment I offered Carol to draw I had no option but to take into account her response—from the first few lines, Carol seemed quite determined to convey some message to me. There is no question of her being consciously aware of *expressing* something in her drawings, but she must have been continuously monitoring my response to each successive drawing. I can only conclude that she felt I was "passing the test", because she continued to draw and tell me the stories for each picture until she came to the letters in the last picture, when she put the pens down in the manner of someone who has finished what she wanted to say.

Mrs C's reaction when I gave my translation of the drawings poses quite a difficult technical problem. Intellectually, she found my ideas absurd, but she was able to respect Carol's reaction to them. Should one ignore this? Or should one praise her for believing in her child? The danger here is the consultant being seen as taking sides with the child against the mother, which makes me tend not to comment on this change of views on the parent's part. I would, however, assume that if Mrs C could accept that Carol was not setting out to defy her, but rather expressing conflicts that she could not cope with, then this may well have led her to offer Carol a different emotional atmosphere when putting her to bed. This change, along with Carol's agreement with my translation of her drawings, enabled her to overcome her unconscious conflicts and the resulting problems.

From a psychoanalytic perspective, Carol's probable aggressive impulses to her mother could be recognized in the manner in which she returned to her first drawing to "inflict" further dots/crabs on her. Another of her drawings seemed to point to fantasies related to pregnancy and probably to hostile impulses related to the birth of her younger sister. If Carol did go into individual therapy, these fantasies would be explored at length, but in the context of this first (and, as I feared, only) meeting, I chose not to mention these possible conflicts.

The findings in this interview would lead me to think that Carol's "impossible behaviour" was strongly linked to the reported conflicts between her parents regarding her disciplining. Ideally, I would recommend that Mr and Mrs C should be seen together to explore the reasons for such disagreements. If these marital meetings could lead the parents to deal with Carol in a more coherent manner, it is quite probable that this would produce an improvement in Carol's behaviour. If this approach was not acceptable to the parents, then some individual work with Carol would certainly be advisable.

This case is presented here as an example of diagnostic interviews where it is clear that the child behaves as if expecting to obtain help from the consultant. Assuming that the follow-up we obtained is reliable, then Carol did manage to escape from her nightmares—many colleagues would argue that, even if this symptom has disappeared, the underlying conflicts still remain and I would entirely agree with this view. However, rightly or wrongly, I felt I had to respond to Carol there and then. The alternative would be to leave aside Carol's pictures and stories and focus on Mrs C's questions, but I was convinced that I would never manage to reassure her regarding Carol's mental health, nor was Mrs C allowing me to obtain sufficient evidence to recognise what exactly made her so worried about Carol. All considered, I decided not to ignore Carol's plea for help.

Mandy

Mandy was twelve years old when she was admitted to the paediatric ward of a general hospital for three weeks, in order to undergo detailed investigations to identify the reason for her "nine-year history of hip pain, starting at the age of three, when she recounts her inability to bear weight on her right leg". At the request of the paediatrician, she was seen by an orthopaedic surgeon and a rheumatologist, but in spite of careful clinical and laboratorial investigations, no definite pathology was identified. A full physiotherapy assessment was requested, and I was asked for a psychiatric opinion.

Mandy looked younger than her actual age. I was told that her academic progress was outstanding and, in fact, she was among the top pupils in her year. Her conversation showed her to be an intelligent girl, but at times her voice and some mannerisms appeared more appropriate for someone several years younger than she was. She had a younger brother, who attended the same school as she did. I was told they had a warm, close relationship.

I first met Mandy in the ward, but she came to see me in my own room a couple of days later, together with her parents. Mandy was a gifted musician, playing several instruments, besides being part of the school choir. Though she said she enjoyed playing sports, she had not actually played any sport for many years. At school and in her daily general life she had developed several coping mechanisms to counterbalance the pain and the various constrained movements that characterised her gait.

At this hospital, the physiotherapist and the occupational therapist had developed a sophisticated team to work with children with orthopaedic problems and their report on Mandy gave a vivid description of her condition.

> Mandy walks with an unusual gait. She does not heel strike with the right foot and has only a very short stance phase on the right. She holds the knee straight and swings the leg through rigidly. However, when asked to stand on the right leg and step over an obstacle with the left, she could maintain stance on the right for several seconds. ... Ankle has full movement. In a non-clinical situation (e.g., dressing/undressing or playing) at least 100% hip flexion was observed, and also 100% knee flexion. On the bicycle, she managed at least 20° active abduction. ... Mandy reported no difficulties in getting dressed and she was able to demonstrate her ability to reach forward and put on her socks and shoes. She had no difficulty getting on and off a chair or toilet and was able to transfer herself in and out of the bath by sitting on the edge, swinging her legs over and lowering herself down and back up. During all these functional activities, Mandy was able to flex her hip fully and although she did tend to hold her right leg straight, we did observe a full range of flexion in her knee during the sessions, usually when she was fully absorbed in an activity.

The final summary put quite concisely the view of all the professionals: "Mandy obviously has some stiffness and weakness in her hip and knee, but this is probably secondary to her abnormal gait".

When I first met Mandy in the ward, I spent some time learning her account of her difficulties. Her mother was also present, but I did not ask her any questions about her life and her views on Mandy's problems. Because Mandy was meant to stay some more days in the hospital, I opted for a longer appointment during one of my clinics there. This would also give me an opportunity to meet Mr M. The three of them came to see me at the arranged time.

Mrs M worked part-time in a social services residential facility. She had trained as a nurse and worked for several years in various settings.

She had greatly enjoyed working in hospitals, but had left this work to devote herself to bringing up her children. When the youngest one started full-time school, Mrs M found a job not far from where she lived and this enabled her to be home when the children returned from school. She was in her late thirties and recounted a happy childhood and good relationships with friends. Mrs M got on well with her parents and siblings, whom she met often.

Mr M had a clerical job in a government department. He occupied a middle position and he told us that he saw his career as quite successful. He was also in his late thirties. Mr M came from a small family, who lived some distance from London, and he said they all got on well with each other. He had always enjoyed good health. He spoke easily and warmly with both his wife and Mandy. My impression was of a man who took great pride in the closeness and warmth of his family, though he made it quite clear that it was his wife who took charge of matters related to the children, particularly so when a question of health was involved.

Mandy's birth and early developmental milestones had been unremarkable. She was described as a happy and healthy baby, who was the big attraction in her wider family, being the first grandchild to be born. But at age three, Mandy complained one day that she felt some pain in her hip. According to Mrs M, the general practitioner examined her and declared that there was nothing wrong. We will never know precisely why Mandy went on complaining of the pain, but she did do so and Mrs M took her to the general practitioner a second and a third time. Again, he said he found no sign of disease, but eventually he requested a white cell count. This seemed to be normal and I imagine he reassured Mrs M that there was no possibility that Mandy might be presenting any form of rheumatic disease. However, the pain must have persisted, because some time later Mandy was referred to the paediatrician. This account was being given to me more than seven years after the events took place, so it is not possible to judge the accuracy of the chronology. The fact is that, at some point, the paediatrician referred Mandy to an orthopaedist for a second opinion and I was told that the latter informed Mandy and her parents that she was suffering from an "irritable hip". Mr and Mrs M discussed this diagnosis with the family doctor and I was told that "he ridiculed such an idea", but it was quite obvious from the parents' account that the general practitioner's words did not reassure them at all.

When I asked Mandy and her parents how her symptoms affected family life, they just could not stop laughing as they recounted innumerable occasions when the ordinary daily home routine involved Mandy in movements and complaints that had now become an integral part of the family's life. It sounded as if they were mocking Mandy, but then they also told me that no sooner did she complain of pain, there would be a flurry of attempts to help her overcome it. If various home remedies could not accomplish this, Mandy had an appointment made with one of the doctors who kept an eye on her progress. At first, I thought that Mandy only had help when she asked for it, but gradually a different picture emerged.

It turned out that each member of the family had a "typical feature" that the others recognised as a sign of distress, discomfort or illness. If Mr M happened to frown his forehead "too intensely", some member of the family would ask him if he had a headache and offer to get him some analgesic tablet. If Mandy's younger brother ever said he did not want to eat because he was not hungry, this was immediately taken as a sign that he was ill, leading to a consideration of what he had eaten in the previous meal and the possibility of requiring appropriate medication. If Mrs M spoke in a harsh tone of voice, the family would ask her if she was experiencing some cramp—"is it that time of the month?" If Mandy sat back on a chair while watching television, with her head bending back, this was an indication that her hip was hurting. Mandy and her parents were roaring in laughter as they recounted this private compendium of medical signs and symptoms—I could not avoid asking whether this catalogue of maladies and remedies was perhaps linked to the fact that Mrs M had worked as a nurse. Mr M agreed and added that his wife had been the original diagnostician for all these pathognomonic signs. She managed to smile, but retorted by blaming the others for not being totally free of physical complaints for any length of time.

I asked Mandy what she made of all the diagnoses and explanations she had been given over the years. She was embarrassed, clearly at a loss for words, and said, with a shrug of her shoulders, "I have an irritable hip". But could she tell me what this meant? She searched for words, and I ventured an explanation that virtually repeated these same words: when she makes some exaggerated movements or when she is very tired, her hip becomes irritated and it hurts. Seeing that these words appeared to produce no visible echo of recognition in her, I thought of asking her to put on paper what she thought was her hip.

Mandy made a picture that surprised me (Figure 29), since it seemed rather immature for her age. She drew herself dressed up and when I

Figure 29. Mandy's first drawing.

asked her to mark her hip, she drew semi-circles to indicate their location. I hesitated about how to proceed and ended up suggesting she
drew herself naked. This picture (Figure 30) seemed even more immature, not only by the lack of any identifying features, but also because
of the way in which Mandy drew her hands and feet. I thought that
she had little awareness of her bodily features, being struck by her not
depicting her face or any elements that might identify the drawing as
showing a girl. Because the context of our meeting was her pain and
consequent difficulties, I decided to ignore these points and I asked her
to show me what she imagined was going on *inside* her joints, to depict
where the pain was actually localised. She drew (Figure 31) a very concrete image of how she visualised her hip joint.

She put some arrows to indicate movement and explained that the
joint was surrounded by soft tissues (i.e., not so hard as the bones that
composed the hip joint).

I tried to discuss with Mandy which movements would bring out
the pain and what did she imagine happened to the joint when she was

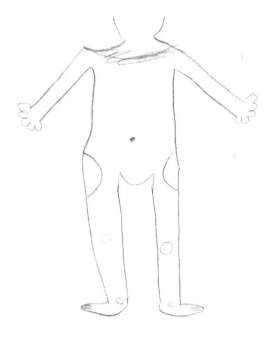

Figure 30. Mandy's second drawing.

resting. From the previous conversation, I had no doubt that Mandy had good intelligence, but when talking about this pain that she had carried for over eight years it was clear she had not managed to construct any meaningful picture of what brought up or alleviated the pains in her "irritable hip". I thought she had come to imagine some sick core of bone tissue that was lodged on the side of her body, deep under the skin, but she seemed totally unable to produce any idea as to what "irritated" this bit of her body, causing all the incapacitating symptoms that she complained about; nor was she very certain of what alleviated these symptoms.

I suggested to Mandy that her family doctor had probably been right all along and that there was no organic pathology in her joint, this being the reason why all the tests had been consistently negative over

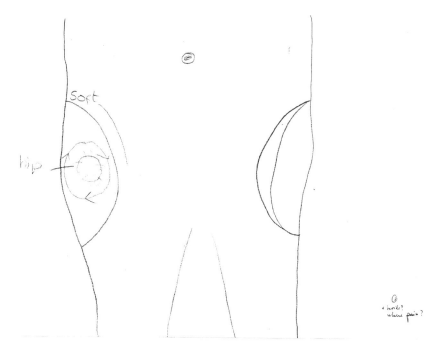

Figure 31. Mandy's third drawing.

the years. I emphasised that I had no doubt that she did feel the pains
and all the difficulties in walking, but I suggested this was caused by
her *fears* of what was going on or what might come to happen inside
her hip, rather than by any actual inflammatory processes in the joint.
I went on to tell her a story that most patients can quickly make sense
of: if you feel a pain and visit a doctor, considering that he will always
make a very careful examination of that part of your body where the
pain is localised, what difference does it make whether he: (i) tells you
he cannot find anything wrong and that you should come back in some
six months' time if the pain recurs; or (ii) he tells you he cannot find
anything wrong, but, "just to be on the safe side", perhaps you should
undergo some tests? Mandy, like the vast majority of patients, promptly
replied that with the second alternative she would feel rather worried
that the doctor might be trying to protect her and hide from her some
pathology he had found during the examination.

When Mandy said this, I turned to Mrs M and said that I had no
doubt that when she took Mandy to see one of her doctors this was,

for her, a measure of caution and care, but I thought there was a strong possibility that this move conveyed to Mandy a confirmation that there was reason to worry about the complaint she had made. Mrs M voiced her disbelief that this might be the case. I reminded her of her nursing training and asked her what precisely did she imagine was the organic damage underlying the diagnosis of "irritable hip"—she laughed and said that, of course, she knew that there was no particular injury to the bones or joints of the hip. So, I asked, how could she explain the image that Mandy had formed of a definite, concrete lesion? Both parents had seen Mandy's drawings, but my question surprised them, as if they had never considered the possibility that Mandy would have formed this concrete idea of actual damage to her joint. Predictably, Mrs M could not explain how Mandy would have arrived at that. I asked if the parents could see any connection between Mandy's image of physical disease and my story about the different responses of a doctor to a patient's complaint. Indeed, they could see that Mandy might have interpreted their reactions as indicating their fear that some damage might be present. I could now ask Mrs M what she thought would have happened if she had responded to Mandy's complaints in line with her knowledge that there was no physical basis for her pain. Mrs M could only raise her hands and shoulders to indicate the impossibility of answering this question with any certainty. Of course, there was no way of putting the clock back, but I suggested that if both Mr and Mrs M were truly to believe that Mandy did not have any physical, organic damage to her hip, they might treat her complaints differently—and it was conceivable that Mandy might, gradually, change her reaction to her pains and her anxiety about her hip joint.

Mandy and her parents left our meeting looking rather bemused; they seemed frustrated that they had not been given a clear, definite medical or psychiatric diagnosis, but they also looked as if they might put my suggestion to the test.

I saw Mandy and her parents again two weeks later. Mandy admitted the pain was "a little better"—it was less troublesome and less incapacitating. Earlier that week, Mandy had seen the physiotherapist, who had found "considerable progress" in Mandy's movements since their first meeting. Mandy and her parents felt very encouraged by this. I asked what had been happening at home. In what seemed to be their typical way of discussing these issues (i.e., making self-deprecating remarks), Mr and Mrs M recounted their struggle each time Mandy stretched out on the TV chair in the "I feel the pain" manner or, worse still, when she actually complained of trouble with walking. They "could hear [themselves] wanting to call the doctor", but then they looked at each other for support and set out to convince Mandy that she should wait a bit longer, just in case the pain became less severe. Initially, Mandy had reacted in a hostile manner, but gradually the parents could perceive signs of ambivalence and reluctant "cooperation". Eventually, they noticed that the intervals between crises of pain had increased.

I saw the family again three weeks later and this time there was a dramatic change in their report. Mandy had not complained of any pain for the past two weeks, and the big news was that she had started to play football at school. We talked about this new situation. Mandy was clearly relieved to find herself no longer thinking of having a "irritable hip", but her parents were still struggling with an anxiety that they might be overlooking some pathology which required attention. We made an appointment for one month later. Mandy saw the rheumatologist later that week and she was given a full discharge, since she no longer had any joint pain and her hip movements were found to be virtually normal. The physiotherapist also saw Mandy, and her tests confirmed that all joint movements were now within normal limits and her gait was normal.

Information we obtained a couple of months later told us that Mandy had not complained of any more pains and that, even though she kept up with her involvement with the musical department at school, she also continued with her football, and now other sports as well.

Comments

I would assume that one or both of Mandy's parents had some anxiety about her health (life?) that was not identified in our meetings. We will never know the precise cause of Mandy's original joint pains when she was three years old, but I would argue that the subsequent progress of this pain represents a response to Mrs M's anxiety. It seems that the family doctor tried hard to reassure Mandy's parents about the girl's complaints, but clearly one or both of them were trying to cope with anxieties that were not addressed.

Even though my interviews did not bring to light the content of Mr and Mrs M's anxiety, it seems that they felt reassured by the progress shown by Mandy. Fortunately, they did not take my comments in a "it's all my fault, then, is it?" manner—instead, they managed to feel that they might help Mandy through responding differently to her complaints. This would mean that they continued to influence each other, but this time in a more positive way.

Fatima

This case is presented because of its most unusual features. Some of its elements are common enough in a paediatric practice, but the cultural aspects affecting the feelings and behaviour of the parents may not be so familiar to many practitioners. I was certainly taken by surprise at various points of our work and, time and again, I had to struggle with the decision of whether I could make a comment of the kind I would use with the majority of my patients or whether I had to consider the existence of religious, cultural, and familial pressures that demanded respect and silence rather than an interpretation of individual unconscious motivations. I was extremely grateful to Mrs F for her patience and her willingness to teach me some of the beliefs she had grown up with.

Fatima was referred to the paediatrician at twenty-one months of age because of her breath-holding attacks. In his referral letter, the general practitioner described that these attacks were the worst ones he had ever seen, in terms of severity and persistence. He had recommended various techniques to the mother on how to deal with Fatima's crises and the health visitor had also tried to reassure the mother and to help her to cope with Fatima, but all to no avail.

The paediatrician examined Fatima very carefully and concluded that she was physically normal and there was no organic basis for her disturbed and disturbing behaviour. After discussing his findings in general terms with Mrs F, he decided to take advantage of the fact that she was a sciences graduate and explained to her the mechanism whereby the concentration of carbon dioxide increases during the breath-holding attacks and this leads to stimulation of the breathing centre and the inevitable eventual resumption of normal breathing—therefore, nothing to be afraid of. Mrs F listened with due respect and attention, but it was obvious that she was not reassured by the rigours of physiology. But this was an unusual paediatrician and he managed to convey to Mrs F that he was *interested* in what made her so anxious, and Mrs F proceeded to give him a picture of her experiences as Fatima's mother.

Fatima had not been a planned child and her birth had forced Mrs F to interrupt, if not give up, her career. Delivery necessitated a Caesarean section and the wound turned septic, creating further problems. Mr and Mrs F were living with her parents at the time (they now lived in a house of their own, though quite close to her parents) and there were many tensions in the house, including a psychotic brother of Mrs F's who, at times, became violent. Fatima proved to be "a difficult baby" and nights were disturbed and demanding. Mrs F admitted to the fact that she had "always been afraid of having children", in case they had some physical abnormality. She had an older child, now eight years old, who "had always been very easy to look after", but Fatima's breath-holding attacks "resulted in mini-deaths" and Mrs F was plainly terrified that Fatima might die. Mrs F painfully summed up her feelings, saying that perhaps she was "temperamentally unsuited" to look after small children.

The paediatrician acknowledged the distress and guilt felt by Mrs F. He wondered whether she might have suffered a puerperal depression, but he had no doubt that she was quite depressed at the time of the interview. He recognised that Mrs F was at the end of her tether and that Fatima was now "ruling her mother, banging her head on hard surfaces because she knows this terrifies her mother, should there be a conflict of will". He explained his views to Mrs F and urged her to accept a referral to the hospital child psychiatrist, who had a special interest in the problems of under-fives. Mrs F was not convinced that this was necessary, but she agreed to "give it a try".

Fatima was brought to see me by both parents. She was a very good-looking, petite, and well-proportioned girl. Huge, black eyes, together with a wide smile that revealed regular, very white teeth, made her a very attractive child—and she seemed well aware of how enchanting she could be. She behaved in an age-appropriate way, smiling at me, but keeping close to her parents' legs as she stood on the floor and examined the toys I had prepared for her arrival. She accepted a doll that I offered her, promptly showing it to her parents after having a close look at it herself. She behaved like an intelligent girl—inquisitive, dextrous, very observant of the attitudes and words of the people around her.

As Fatima engaged in her play with some toys, I asked the parents to describe her symptoms. Mr F allowed his wife to tell me of Fatima's breath-holding attacks and her occasional episodes of banging her head against the floor or some wall. Mr F explained that he spent little time at home, so that he had not witnessed the more intensely disturbing episodes of Fatima's behaviour, but he was keen to support his wife's account. In spite of his words, I had a strong impression that Mr F was not as anxious as his wife about their daughter's symptoms. I asked the parents to give me an idea of their backgrounds.

Mr F was in his early forties, a senior professional occupying a good job in a large firm. His family were all still in the East and it was obvious that he saw his wife and children as the main centre of his life. He professed to be on good terms with his wife's family, but this appeared to be based on shared cultural values, rather than on affective ties. A quiet and gentle man, Mr F had come to recognise his inability to comfort or reassure his wife.

Mrs F was in her early thirties. After obtaining a sciences degree, she had changed to an administrative career, where she gained quick promotion to a very senior position. Her family had a complex structure and its details only emerged over the course of several interviews. At this first meeting, I was only told of the ages and social positions of her siblings, including the mentally ill older brother and an older sister, who both lived at home with the parents.

After their marriage twelve years earlier, Mr and Mrs F lived for six months with Mrs F's parents and then bought their own flat, not too far away from them. Out of the five children, Mrs F had always been her mother's closest confidante and supporter—a role she continued to play after getting married. The couple decided to wait until she finished her studies before they had their first child. This first daughter had had sleeping problems and Mrs F had found this difficult to handle, but the girl had developed normally, with no significant problems.

Throughout this account, Fatima had been playing with toys, turning to either parent for an occasional word or gesture of comfort and they responded each time, quietly, lovingly, and unobtrusively. I thought these were intelligent, sensitive parents who had given their daughter the kind of care that had led Fatima to love and trust them. At no point did I pick up signs of anxiety in either parent—except when there was the remotest possibility that Fatima might be exposing herself to some danger. When Fatima tried to lift a heavy bucket (full of toys), Mrs F jumped forward to help her; the same reaction followed when Fatima moved near a chair that was close to a window, and also when she tried to climb on a chair. Looking at me, Mrs F was clearly embarrassed, but she explained that each of these moves made her dread an accident, which might lead to a breath-holding attack—and, as might be predicted, Mrs F told me that Fatima was not allowed to ride a bicycle or play with some toys that were considered "dangerous".

I decided that Fatima and her mother were caught up in a vicious circle, where each was reacting to the other's behaviour, and I felt that, whatever had been the cause of Fatima's early "attacks", she was now reacting to her mother's anxiety and dread. I explained my hypothesis to Mr and Mrs F. I would not be able to give them a reason, a cause for Fatima's breath holding when it first happened, but I suspected that it had occurred in circumstances which might have led Mrs F to interpret Fatima's behaviour in such a way that the episode became a threat—a warning of something which might recur and bring serious consequences. Both parents looked puzzled and their faces showed their efforts to retain an attitude of respect and politeness. I asked Mrs F to take herself back to that first episode when Fatima's behaviour caused her to be afraid. After some insistence on my part, Mrs F reluctantly told me of a time when Fatima was ten months old and she was about to give her a bath. The older daughter was helping Mrs F while she was preparing the water. Fatima herself was lying on a mat, on the floor, near a bed.

Mrs F had her back to Fatima when she suddenly heard a thud. She turned round and saw Fatima crying, lying on her back on the floor. It occurred to her that Fatima had lifted herself, holding on to the edge of the bed, but her hands had slipped and she had fallen down (she later discovered that it had been the older sister who had put Fatima on the bed, even though she had always forbidden her from lifting the baby). Mrs F rushed to pick Fatima up and this was when Fatima "went blue".

But why should this episode lead Mrs F to dread its repetition? I commented that Mrs F might have easily seen that event as no more than an isolated accident—probably, she would have rationally understood it to be a regrettable accident, but no more than this. So if, instead, she came to interpret it as a worrying warning, then presumably she must have been influenced by some factor that we had not yet recognised.

After much thought and further encouragement from me, Mrs F told me how, at the moment when she saw "Fatima turning blue", she thought: "My God! I have done something awful and God is taking her away from me!" She was clearly embarrassed by saying this, but she explained that the embarrassment lay not only in the telling me about that thought, but also in the fact that she could recognise that such a sentiment clashed with all her views of life, death, and religion. It gradually emerged that Mrs F had, some months earlier, complained to her mother about Fatima's sleeping problems and, much to her surprise, her mother had suddenly told her that she was being ungrateful for God's gift; this child had been entrusted to her by God and she was meant to care for her and enjoy her, or else He would take her back. Finally, having told me this, Mrs F was laughing, claiming that, of course, she never believed in such a threat. There had been many other occasions when Mrs F felt so exasperated that she had actually wished she had not had Fatima, but, she argued, these were "normal" emotional outbursts, where words are not meant to be taken literally.

There was no point in arguing with Mrs F. I could only repeat that the dreaded thought *had* occurred to her that God might take Fatima away—and it was possible, if not likely, that such a belief still lay behind her anxiety that Fatima might die. At the time of this interview, I was running a group for under-fives and their parents, and I suggested to Mrs F that perhaps she might bring Fatima to our meetings, as that would give us an opportunity not only to discuss these problems further, but also to observe how Fatima behaved in the company of other children. Mrs F did not like this suggestion, saying she would not feel comfortable in a group situation. In view of her decision, we arranged another appointment.

We met again 3 weeks later. "Nothing has changed", Mrs F announced. She told me of discussions with her husband (who was not present this time) over the points that had emerged in our first meeting. It sounded as if Mr F had decided not to miss the wood for the trees and had focused his arguments on the idea that the best they ought to do was to move house, so that they would live further away from Mrs F's mother. Fatima was playing with some toys in the room and Mrs F seemed happy to tell me more about her involvement with her family. What she went on to tell me was not coming from her unconscious; rather, she told me of experiences that were part of ordinary daily life for her, but each datum surprised me and I had to ask for explanations, since I was not familiar with the patterns of family relationships that governed Mrs F's life.

Mrs F's two older siblings had come to live with family relations in this country in their late teens. When Mrs F and her parents came to Britain, those two continued to live with the relatives, in order not to interrupt their studies and also to give the family time to settle down. About one year later, one of those two, an older sister, wanted to marry a young man of her choice and their father forbade her from doing this—and she decided never to marry anyone else. As this sister moved into her thirties, she became increasingly bitter, complaining of the futility of her life. For her, I learnt, it was a reason for great shame that she had not married and had not given birth to children. Somehow, at some point, it became clear that Mrs F was expected to have a child that her sister could bring up. Mrs F felt that, having one daughter alive and well, she wanted to carry on with her career and not have any more children, but her mother and other relations put pressure on her to change her mind. Eventually, Mrs F gave in and fell pregnant, whereupon her sister gave up her job in preparation to bring up the new child.

When the baby arrived, but turned out to cry so much and to make so many demands during the night, the transfer of the child was delayed. When Fatima started her breath-holding attacks and "threatening to die", the aunt bought herself a flat and found another job. I eventually grasped the complexity of the situation; one of the bewildering details was the fact that there was no question of Mrs F feeling resentment or anger towards her mother or sister, since she claimed that the family's customs were part of her own ethos and she saw it as her duty to comply with them. Sadly, Mrs F's despair was such, and her helplessness vis-à-vis her family was so intense, that she had occasionally spoken aloud of her resentment that Fatima was alive, since this is what kept the whole problem unresolved. Again, her mother had taken this as a literal wish and a provocation of God's wrath.

Mrs F could recognise that she thought her sister's position still ambivalent, but as long as Fatima went on with her attacks Mrs F did not need to force a confrontation and a decision. On the other hand, if the attacks stopped, she would have to declare Fatima available and feel herself a rejecting mother, whether the sister accepted the girl or not. But we had reached an impasse. I was postulating the existence of feelings that affected Mrs F and led her to attitudes which were perceived by Fatima as a justification or cause for fear and panic—and as Fatima displayed her panic in the form of breath-holding attacks, Mrs F again felt justified in her dread. But, repeatedly, Mrs F claimed that she did not harbour any negative feelings towards her mother, her sister, or God—to her, it was indisputable that Fatima suffered from some condition that might damage her or even kill her. I tried to interpret the dynamics of the situation between the two sisters, saying that Mrs F had no room for manoeuvre: if Fatima became normal, she would find herself forced to offer to give her up and this might be making her wish that the attacks continued; or, if she decided that she did not want to part with Fatima, this would expose her to criticism from her mother and others. Mrs F was an intelligent woman and she could grant me that these were plausible readings of her predicament, but she would time and again return to the same refrain of "something wrong in Fatima". Rightly or wrongly, I thought, I would not manage to help Mrs F on the basis of searching to convey insight; perhaps if we could count on more interviews, this might become feasible, but I could not believe Mrs F would give me many more chances of helping her through our discussions. I tried, therefore, to persuade Mrs F to come with Fatima to our group meetings.

The group for under-fives met once each week for two hours. Fathers only attended very seldom. We had a variety of toys and games available, and the mothers sat around the room while the children played with each other or on their own. We were four professionals attending the whole meeting and we had between three and five children at each meeting. Halfway through the session, the children were given biscuits and a drink, which brought them to sit round a table and "socialise" with each other. During this break, I took the mothers to another room, where we could discuss any topics they raised. Most times, one of the mothers would bring up some difficulty she experienced with her child and this allowed the other mothers to make comparisons, give opinions, exchange views, etc.

My hope was that Mrs F might be "forced" to observe Fatima in a totally unfamiliar setting, where other mothers and the professional staff might help her to see Fatima from a different perspective. After much reluctance, she accepted it.

Fatima had no difficulty making herself at home. For the first half of her first visit, she stayed either on her mother's lap or stood on the floor, but remained very close to her mother's knees. Gradually, she moved towards the toys lying around the room. We had some three tricycles in the room, but the moment Fatima moved towards one of them, Mrs F dashed off in her direction, trying to convince her to play with something else. The same reaction appeared if Fatima went near the window or built too high a tower of bricks. Predictably, at one of these interventions, another mother asked Mrs F why she was intervening in Fatima's play, and gradually a discussion developed over the risks that children needed to face, so as to learn how to master various situations. Mrs F could now only hint at the intensity of her fears, rather stressing Fatima's symptom and the ease with which some trivial accident could trigger it off.

When the breaks came and I called the mothers to join me in another room, Mrs F found this quite intolerable. Her ambivalence was painfully visible and I am sure she made herself move away to save face with the other mothers. When we sat down away from the children, Mrs F could barely concentrate on the conversation. She was desperately listening out for any cries that would signify Fatima needing her help. She never managed to voice the kind of anxieties that she had told me in private and only very briefly, in the course of the general meeting, did Mrs F ask me about any possible medical condition that might be afflicting Fatima. I asked her about the family situation and she told me that her sister had now decided to devote herself to her job. On the one hand, this freed Mrs F from the obligation to yield Fatima to her, but it still left her to cope with her anxieties over Fatima's physical fitness.

As was bound to happen, each time we finished our "mothers' meeting" and returned to the children's room, Mrs F found Fatima playing happily with another child or with a member of staff. This meant that, at each meeting we had, Fatima was allowed to take "bigger risks". The turning point came when Mrs F discovered that Fatima was quite proficient at operating the pedals of one of the tricycles, without any harm following.

After some weeks, Mrs F had to admit that Fatima had not presented any more episodes of breath-holding or of head-banging. She was also sleeping without much difficulty and there had been a change in the family atmosphere that Mrs F welcomed, but still felt she could not explain or understand. Perhaps it was Mrs F's scientific mind that accepted the evidence that disproved her theory over Fatima's health, or perhaps it was her maternal instincts that gradually led her to accept or even claim her right to mother Fatima. I was sure that her sister's formal renouncement of the original contract played a very central role in Mrs F's changed attitude to Fatima, but observing Fatima's growing ability to fend for herself and to move away from her mother must have also helped Mrs F to recognise that she could "own" Fatima—a perfectly normal, lovely little daughter.

Comments

Mrs F kept in touch with me for several months and she reported that Fatima had not presented any further difficulties. As stated in the introduction, this case was described because of its uncommon features. However, it does illustrate the extent to which a child can present serious symptoms as a response to anxiety generated by the child's inability to comprehend the nature of the mother's excessive protective, controlling, restrictive behaviour. Our psychoanalytic literature speaks of "fears of annihilation" and similar unconscious fantasies where the child presumably experiences a sense of dread which we adults might link to a fear of dying, but we do not seem to appreciate how often these anxieties constitute a *response*—not to the child's "death instincts" or similar constructs, but to the exposure to a loved figure whose expression of anxiety cannot be understood by the child.

Fatima's pathological behaviour disappeared and, to the best of my knowledge, this can only be attributed to the fundamental change in the way that Mrs F treated her. Whatever instincts operated in her unconscious, they must have remained unaltered. This type of successful intervention underlines the usefulness of looking not only into the child's *internal* world, but also into the world where the child develops, from which the child gains the input that forms its eventual internal world.

Daniel*

Daniel was 13 months old when his parents agreed to see a child psychiatrist out of desperation. Daniel was biting "everyone around him". They had tried to find some logic behind the biting, with no success. Daniel's choice of people to bite appeared to show no discernible pattern; if most occasions followed "signs of anger or frustration", there were other times when Daniel would bite someone with no recognisable emotional affect.

Daniel's parents were young professionals. Mrs D's pregnancy and labour had been normal and Daniel was developing normally. He walked reasonably well, he understood very well words addressed to him, his articulation seemed clear, and his vocabulary was increasing in an age-appropriate manner. While his parents sat down and talked to me, Daniel made his way to a desk where I kept a dolls' house, toys, pens, and paper and started to play with various toys in a manner that demonstrated good coordination and an appreciation of the function of each toy. He handled the toys gently and at one point asked his father to pick him up. He seemed to pay attention to the flow of our

---

*Previously published in *Untying the Knot* (Brafman, 2001).

conversation, but he did not appear controlling or demanding; instead, having his desire satisfied, he now nestled his head quietly and lovingly into his father's shoulder, as if respecting the fact that his father was conversing with a stranger.

Mr and Mrs D told me of the multitude of colleagues, friends, relations, health visitors, and doctors, who had given them advice on how to help Daniel to stop his biting. Among other things, they had told him off, they had hit him, bitten him back, put strong-flavoured substances on his lips, put him in his cot, strapped him on his chair, etc.—all to no avail. I was quite convinced, from their account, that they did not really believe that I would ever manage to divine any new miraculous technique that would be of use.

Considering Daniel's behaviour towards the toys, his parents, and myself, I was certain that this was an eminently educable, responsive child; his parents had clearly enabled him to deal with himself and the world with respect and consideration—with the glaring exception of his biting. My conclusion was that Daniel's biting had met some blind spot in his parents' view of the world or, to put it more correctly, their view of how Daniel should relate to people around him. It followed that I should explore each parent's background and their attitudes about the biting.

Mrs D was a Jewish American young woman who had moved to England after her marriage. She had been an active participant in the social movements of the sixties. Overtly, she rejected ordinary conventions and she had married Mr D against her parents' wishes—though not religious, he came from an Irish Catholic family. However, some hesitations in her answers and the occasional change in the tone of her voice made me think that these could be indications that, for her, the transgression of customs and conventions might lead to conflict and perhaps even guilt. Mr D was the same age as his wife. He came to England for his university studies and made a successful career here. He believed that a new society was needed, that previous generations must have failed if the Cold War and Vietnam had followed the previous World War. His childhood and adolescence had taught him that "survival and well-being were [his own] responsibility". He was very conscious of the sense of loyalty to family and friends, but like his wife, he argued for each individual's right to fight for himself.

Carefully, but with determination, I asked each parent to comment on Daniel's biting. Specifically, following my previous findings, I wanted them to concentrate on the issue of a child's duties to his elders and his rights to establish his own identity. It must be noted that I was taking advantage of the fact that these were parents who had given these issues considerable thought, even if not explicitly in terms of the upbringing of their beloved firstborn.

Mrs D felt that a child was entitled to try and gain possession of things he desired, but she also believed that a child had to learn to moderate his desires and accept that others also had wishes and rights. To some extent, Mr D could agree with this formulation, but he firmly believed that a child must not be allowed to learn that surrender and compliance are the rule of the world. They could both understand the concept of compromise, but as they focused on a growing child—their son—Mrs D felt that biting was a personal attack that transgressed the other person's integrity, whilst her husband believed that if his son had no other weapon at his disposal, then biting was a legitimate means of defence and self-assertion.

I translated all this for Mr and Mrs D: they were criticising, reprimanding, punishing, and disciplining Daniel, probably even using similar or the same words. However, each of them had very conflicting views about their son's behaviour. Mrs D was trying to bring up a child who was not bound to the Jewish values she professed to have left behind, but her injunctions that he stopped biting others were essentially based precisely on those values. For his part, Mr D insisted Daniel stopped biting, but he deeply believed that if Daniel was to obey him, he might develop into the kind of human being which Mr D despised—someone incapable of asserting his rights and fighting for his wishes.

Not surprisingly, Mr and Mrs D, in virtual unison, told me I was talking nonsense. I was reading too much into what they had said, I was drawing inferences which they could admit were plausible, but of no relevance to the issue of their son's behaviour. They were trying hard to retain their politeness. I told them that I could not offer any proof of the validity of my interpretation, but I insisted that the only thing they could do to help Daniel was to discuss their views, as they had emerged in our meeting. I enumerated a long list of Daniel's behaviours during the meeting which were evidence of the many ways in which they had taught him to develop as a well-functioning child—all of which suggested that Daniel must be picking up from their words and behaviour about the biting that the overt message contained an underlying *covert* one that contradicted it, and this left him feeling confused about their *real, actual* expectations of him.

Mr and Mrs D refused my suggestion of a further appointment. They offered me the polite compromise of a telephone call to report on progress. A few days later I received a call from Mrs D: she was amused, apologetic, and immensely puzzled—since the moment they left my room, Daniel had not bitten anyone again. She did not know how this could possibly have happened, she said.

Comments

Contrary to the other cases in this book, I cannot say much about Daniel's unconscious ideas regarding his position in the world. We only have the evidence of his behaviour during my consultation and of the account his parents gave of his behaviour in daily life. This is behaviour that, from a psychoanalytic perspective, we would consider evidence of exaggerated hostile impulses, manifesting themselves though oral mechanisms; it is quite possible that the expression "oral sadistic" might be brought up, since Daniel was using his teeth as weapons against those around him, even if he could perceive the feedback that these others were being hurt by his bites.

It would be impossible to establish what was on Daniel's mind when he bit someone for the first time, but as happens with many other children, an incidental piece of behaviour is somehow transformed into a habit—and by the time these children come to see us, we are supposed to make sense of a piece of behaviour which is not acceptable to parents or the world at large. But how are we to interpret such behaviour? Is it proof of faulty development of sociability? Could it indicate a lack of awareness of the distinction between different objects? Is this early evidence of later pathology? As argued in other parts of this book, this diagnostic evaluation will depend entirely on the conceptual framework of the professional seeing the child. I took the line that Daniel was *responding* to a confusing injunction from his parents—this evaluation relies on seeing Daniel and his parents as part of a mutually influencing system of interactions, where a change in this interaction can bring about further changes in the other participants of the inter-relating system.

According to the referrer, he was not consulted for further problems regarding Daniel. Unfortunately, I cannot report further follow-up contact with the D family, but it seems that the crisis that brought them to the consultation was overcome successfully.

Peter

This is a brief account that shows how a parent's feelings and behaviour can influence the emotional development of the child, but it is described here because of its most unusual features.

Peter was a twelve-year-old boy who was presenting odd behaviour both at home and in the community. It was the school that decided the boy required a psychological assessment. The educational psychologist diagnosed psychotic behaviour and the boy was referred to the child guidance clinic. When I saw him, Peter addressed me as any other normal young adolescent might do. But, on further inquiry, he told me that at times he would "see" distortions in people and things around him, and also find ideas that he knew were absurd "taking over" his thoughts, making him believe he was going crazy, and this produced further intense anxious feelings. He was seeing me with his mother. They came from an Oriental country and were devoted practitioners of their religion. They led a perfectly normal life and were well settled into the local community. I was finding it quite difficult to make sense of Peter's "hallucinations", since his description of these appeared to be so discordant with the general picture of his personality. As the interview was coming to an end, the mother asked to see me on her own.

Mrs P wanted to tell me that her son's problems had started some months after his circumcision. Following the surgical procedure, in line with the surgeon's recommendations, twice a day she would wash and clean the boy's prepuce. But this was many months earlier and she had continued to perform this cleaning, even if she could see that the skin had healed perfectly. And she asked whether she was justified in continuing to do it. As gently as possible, I told her she should stop doing it.

Follow-up information was that the psychotic behaviour disappeared and, when I offered another appointment, I was given their thanks but told that no further meetings were necessary.

Mark

Mark was just under three years old when he was referred to see me at the child guidance clinic. His father and paternal grandmother brought him to our meeting. Mark greeted me with a smile and quickly made himself at home. He struck me as an intelligent and articulate boy, who happily chose various toys he wanted to play with, and while he appeared to follow the adults' conversation, at no point did he seem to wish to add or correct anything we said.

Mr M and his mother told me of their puzzlement and worry over Mark's behaviour. He frequently vomited food he had just eaten. Mrs M could not understand or make sense of Mark's "provocative, manipulative behaviour", refusing to eat the food she served him unless and until it was presented in a particular manner. Mr M was determined to protect and please his son, but he also found it difficult to meet Mark's expectations and demands. I was also told that whenever they decided to leave home for a walk to the park, Mark would cling to them and, in fact, he virtually refused to play with other children. They had considered placing him a nursery, but Mark reacted with tears and held on to them.

Mark had certainly lived through very traumatic experiences. He was only one year old when his parents split up, and not long afterwards his

159

mother brought another man to live with them. This turned out to be a very violent person and Mark sometimes referred to seeing this man beating up his mother. Social services became involved and, eventually, Mr M, who was living with his mother, was given custody of Mark. When they came to see me, Mr M had just bought a new house not far from his mother's place.

Considering the account of their daily life, I suggested to Mr and Mrs M that Mark appeared to be afraid that they might also "dispose" of him, that he might lose them just as he had lost his mother. This was like opening a Pandora's box: they proceeded to give me innumerable examples of Mark panicking whenever he feared one of them might move away from him.

I put it to Mr and Mrs M that they should try and ignore the past and, instead, treat Mark as a normal child. It was impossible to establish exactly how Mark had experienced being removed from his mother, and it was equally unknown what precisely had led to his first episode of vomiting—but the reaction he now saw in his father and grandmother might have led him to an unconscious belief that this was what ensured that they would care and look after him. I suggested to them that as soon as they spotted signs of distress in Mark they should stop and attempt to urge him to explain what was bothering him—this type of comforting might avoid the boy's anxiety mounting to the point of "needing" to vomit.

I offered the Ms a further appointment, but because of the problems raised by the purchase of the new house, Mr M suggested that he would report on any progress and, if necessary, we could arrange a new meeting. Mr M phoned the clinic one week later: Mark had not had any further episodes of vomiting and the whole atmosphere in the house seemed to have improved. Mrs M felt particularly happy with the new, easier way of relating to her grandson.

Comments

I see this case as a clear, neat illustration of a child "discovering" a symptom that brings from his carers a response that can relieve his underlying anxieties, however much it, sadly, perpetuates a painful, pathological behaviour. Once carers find an effective way of reassuring the child and the child understands the meaning of his symptom, we see a definite improvement of their relationship—and a disappearance of the presenting symptom.

Summing Up

I'm delighted the problem is behind us and that we got some insight into his difficulties, rather than just imposing socially acceptable behaviour over his worries.

—*Claude's mother, Mrs C* (p. XX)

These were very gratifying words. Many of the parents of the children described in this book did express their appreciation for the help their child had obtained, but what most surprised and puzzled them was how this had been achieved; they had never expected their child to have such a capacity to express their thoughts and feelings, their "hidden" anxieties: a new discovery, they felt. From the professional's viewpoint, this reaction shows how many parents will tend to approach their child with words of advice and only too rarely with questions aiming to learn of the child's experience of a particular situation.

As described in the introduction to this book, the vast majority of children who develop physical symptoms with no underlying organic pathology will respond to words of reassurance or various technical approaches. But we do find children and adolescents who have a strong, subtle, and complex bond to one or both parents and when these youngsters develop an overwhelming anxiety; they seek not merely relief, but also their parents' understanding of what they are experiencing. It is this combination of a physical problem and a deep emotional bond with one or both parents that lead me to define the symptom as the expression of a "language of distress", a manner to convey to the parent(s) the child's need to be understood and helped.

The parents cannot but approach the child in line with their reading of the child's words and behaviour—if their interpretation of the child's communication is a correct appraisal of the child's anxiety, all is well and the problem will be resolved. If, however, the parents' response does not meet the child's emotional experience, the child is likely to react in a manner that raises the parents' sense of their child having "something wrong" in him/her which the parents are not managing to help with, and soon we have a vicious circle where both child and parents feel misunderstood and increasingly distressed. We can find this pattern appearing when the child worries about the function of a particular part of his body, but we also find children whose unconscious anxiety is not linked to their physical self, and this can find expression through phobias, nightmares, or other behavioural symptoms.

When a family needs to be referred to a child and adolescent psychiatrist, this will clearly mean that other approaches have failed. Rather than trying to find "the right advice", I have described an approach where *understanding the meaning* of the child's symptom is the objective of the consultation. Because I believe the persistence of the symptom is probably linked to the child's interaction with one or both his parents, I also try to investigate how they had interpreted their child's symptoms and, consequently, have been dealing with the child's problem prior to seeing me. When the parents realise what has, in fact, been tormenting their child and manage to change their approach to him or her, it is almost certain that the child's symptoms will disappear.

REFERENCES

Aunola, K., & Nurmi, J. E. (2005). The role of parenting styles in children's problem behavior. *Child Development, 76*: 1144–1159.

Baker, S. S., Liptak, G. S., & Coletti, R. B. (2006). Constipation guideline committee of the North American Society for Pediatric Gastroenterology, Hepatology and Nutrition. Evaluation and treatment of constipation in infants and children: recommendations of the North American Society for Pediatric Gastroenterology, Hepatology and Nutrition. *Journal of Pediatric Gastroenterology and Nutrition, 43(3):* e1–e13.

Brafman, A. H. (2001). *Untying the Knot.* London: Karnac.

Campbell, A. (4 May 2013). *Six childcare gurus who have changed parenting.* BBC News Magazine. Retrieved from www.bbc.co.uk/news/magazine-22397457 [last accessed 13 October 2015].

Edgcumbe, R. (1978). The psychoanalytic view of the development of encopresis. *Bulletin of the Anna Freud Centre, 1(1):* 57–61.

Farnam, A., Rafeey, M., Farhang, S., & Khodjastejafari, S. (2009). Functional constipation in children: does maternal personality matter? *Italian Journal of Pediatrics, 35(25):* 1–4.

Kushnir J., & Sadeh, A. (2012). Assessment of brief interventions for night-time fears in preschool children. *European Journal of Pediatrics, 171(1):* 67–75.

Spock, B. (1946). *The Common Sense Book of Baby and Child Care*. New York: Duell, Sloan, and Pearce.

van Dijk, M., de Vries, G. J., Last, B. F., Benninga, M. A., & Grootenhuis, M. A. (2015). Parental child-rearing attitudes are associated with functional constipation in childhood. *Archives of Disease in Childhood, 100(4)*: 320–333.

Winnicott, D. W. (1960). Ego distortion in terms of true and false self. In: *The Maturational Processes and the Facilitating Environment*. London: The Hogarth Press.

Winnicott, D. W. (1991). *The Child, the Family and the Outside World*. London: Penguin Books.

INDEX